SARA L. WESTON

The Introvert's Dilemma: Misunderstood and Unique

Contents

Preface   v

1   Chapter 1   1

   Introduction   1

   1.1 Defining Introversion   2

   1.2 Introverts vs. Extroverts   4

   1.3 Introvert Traits and Characteristics   8

   1.4 The Power of Introversion   12

2   Chapter 2   16

   The Introverts Inner World   16

   2.1 The Introvert's Mind   16

   2.2 Introvert's Need for Solitude   19

   2.3 Introvert's Reflection and Introspection   22

   2.4 Introvert's Creativity and Imagination   25

3   Chapter 3   30

   Navigating Social Interactions   30

   3.1 Introverts and Small Talk   30

   3.2 Introverts in Group Settings   33

   3.3 Introverts and Networking   37

   3.4 Introverts and Public Speaking   41

   3.5 Introverts and Social Anxiety   44

4   Chapter 4   48

   The Introverts Relationships   48

   4.1 Introverts in Romantic Relationships   48

   4.2 Introverts and Friendships   52

4.3 Introverts and Family Dynamics   55

4.4 Introverts and Work Relationships   59

5   Chapter 5   63

Embracing Introversion   63

5.1 Self-Acceptance as an Introvert   63

5.2 Setting Boundaries and Prioritizing Self-Care   67

5.3 Finding Balance in an Extroverted World   70

5.4 Harnessing the Strengths of Introversion   74

6   Chapter 6   78

Overcoming Challenges   78

6.1 Dealing with Misunderstandings and Stereotypes   78

6.2 Managing Overstimulation and Burnout   81

6.3 Building Confidence as an Introvert   85

6.4 Navigating Career Challenges as an Introvert   88

7   Chapter 7   93

Thriving as an Introvert   93

7.1 Creating an Introvert-Friendly Environment   93

7.2 Finding Meaningful Connections   97

7.3 Developing a Personal Growth Plan   101

7.4 Celebrating Introversion   104

8   Chapter 8   108

The Future for Introversion   108

8.1 Introverts in a Changing World   108

8.2 The Rise of Introvert Empowerment   111

8.3 Introverts as Leaders and Innovators   115

8.4 The Importance of Introvert Advocacy   118

About the Author   122

Preface

"Look! you're not like everyone else, you're very self con-
tained."

A partner once said this to me during a heated discussion and
many years after we'd separated, I still had those words ringing
in my ears. It lead to a lot of confusion for me about what she
meant. Was it something positive about me, or did she mean
that it was something negative about me, that led us to be in
conflict during our relationship. I began to wonder if there was
something 'wrong' with me that needed fixing. Many years
down the road I discovered that I was an introvert. I didn't
need fixing at all. I'm resourceful, resilient, and incredibly
comfortable at home on my own.

It's my hope that readers of this book, find acceptance in their
introversion and begin to thrive. "The Introvert's Dilemma"
is a celebration of diversity, an ode to the introverted spirit,
and a guide to navigating a world that may not always speak
the language of solitude. By understanding the intricacies of
introversion, we can pave the way for a more inclusive and
harmonious world where both introverts and extroverts coexist
and thrive, recognizing the beauty in the tapestry of human
temperament.

May this book serve as a lantern for those who tread the path
of introversion, illuminating the richness and depth that lies
within, and may it be a bridge that fosters understanding and

appreciation between introverts and extroverts alike.

1

Chapter 1

Introduction

This book delves into the defining characteristics of introversion and highlights the differences between introverts and extroverts. It explores the power and strengths of introversion, emphasizing the unique qualities that introverts possess.

The book takes readers on a journey into the inner world of introverts, exploring their minds, their need for solitude, and their capacity for deep reflection and introspection. It also delves into the creative and imaginative nature of introverts, showcasing how these traits contribute to their unique perspectives and contributions to the world.

Navigating social interactions can be a challenge for introverts, and this book provides valuable insights and strategies for introverts to thrive in various social settings. From small talk to networking and public speaking, the book offers practical advice for introverts to overcome social anxiety and make meaningful connections.

"The Introvert's Dilemma" also explores the dynamics of relationships for introverts, including romantic relationships, friendships, and family dynamics. It addresses the challenges introverts face in work relationships and provides guidance on how to navigate these situations effectively.

Embracing introversion is a key theme in the book, with a focus on self-acceptance, setting boundaries, and prioritizing self-care. It offers strategies for finding balance in an extroverted world and harnessing the strengths of introversion. The book also addresses common challenges faced by introverts, such as dealing with misunderstandings and stereotypes, managing overstimulation and burnout, building confidence, and navigating career challenges.

With a forward-looking perspective, "The Introvert's Dilemma" explores the future of introversion and the rise of introvert empowerment. It highlights the importance of introverts as leaders and innovators and advocates for introvert advocacy. The book concludes by celebrating introversion and encouraging readers to create introvert-friendly environments, find meaningful connections, and develop personal growth plans.

1.1 Defining Introversion

Introversion is a personality trait that is often misunderstood and overlooked in today's extroverted society. It is a characteristic that is commonly associated with being shy, quiet, or socially awkward. However, introversion is much more complex than these surface-level stereotypes. In order to truly understand introversion, we must delve deeper into its definition and explore the unique qualities that introverts possess.

At its core, introversion is a preference for solitude and internal reflection. Introverts gain energy from spending time alone and engaging in activities that allow them to recharge their mental and emotional batteries. This does not mean that introverts dislike social interactions or lack social skills. Rather, introverts simply have a different way of processing and responding to stimuli in their environment.

Introverts tend to be more introspective and thoughtful, often preferring to think before they speak or act. They are known for their ability to listen attentively and observe their surroundings with great detail. This introspective nature allows introverts to have a deep understanding of themselves and the world around them.

Contrary to popular belief, introversion is not synonymous with shyness. While some introverts may also be shy, shyness is a separate trait characterized by fear or anxiety in social situations. Introverts, on the other hand, may enjoy socializing but may find it draining after a certain period of time. They may prefer smaller, more intimate gatherings or one-on-one interactions where they can engage in meaningful conversations.

It is important to note that introversion is not a flaw or a weakness. It is simply a different way of processing information and interacting with the world. Introverts have unique strengths and qualities that should be celebrated and embraced. They often possess a deep sense of empathy, creativity, and analytical thinking.

In a society that values extroversion and constant social engagement, introverts can often feel misunderstood or out of place. They may be labeled as aloof, antisocial, or even arrogant simply because they do not conform to the extroverted ideal. This misunderstanding can lead to feelings of isolation and self-doubt.

However, it is crucial to recognize that introversion is a valid and valuable personality trait. It is estimated that introverts make up approximately one-third to one-half of the population, highlighting the importance of understanding and appreciating introversion in our society.

By defining introversion and shedding light on its unique characteristics, we can begin to challenge the misconceptions and stereotypes surrounding introverts. It is essential to create a more inclusive and accepting environment that values and respects the diversity of personality types.

In the following chapters, we will explore the various aspects of introversion in greater detail. We will delve into the introvert's inner world, their navigation of social interactions, their relationships, and the challenges they face. We will also discuss strategies for embracing introversion, overcoming obstacles, and thriving as an introvert in an extroverted world.

Through this journey, we hope to provide a comprehensive understanding of introversion and empower introverts to embrace their true selves. It is time to celebrate the unique strengths and perspectives that introverts bring to the table and recognize the importance of introvert advocacy in shaping a more inclusive future.

1.2 Introverts vs. Extroverts

Introversion and extroversion are two contrasting personality traits that describe how individuals interact with the world around them. While both introverts and extroverts are part of the same spectrum, they have distinct differences in their preferences, energy sources, and social behaviors. Understanding these differences is crucial in recognizing and appreciating the unique qualities of introverts.

1.2.1 Energy Sources: Introverts and Extroverts

One of the fundamental differences between introverts and extroverts lies in their energy sources. Extroverts tend to gain energy from external stimuli and social interactions. They thrive in lively and stimulating environments, often seeking out social gatherings and engaging in conversations. Extroverts feel recharged and energized by being around people and external activities.

On the other hand, introverts derive their energy from within themselves. They need solitude and quiet time to recharge and regain their mental and emotional energy. Introverts often feel drained after prolonged social interactions and require alone time to reflect and recharge. This doesn't mean that introverts dislike socializing or lack social skills; rather, they have a limited capacity for social interactions and need to balance it with periods of solitude.

1.2.2 Social Preferences: Introverts and Extroverts

Introverts and extroverts also differ in their social preferences. Extroverts are naturally outgoing and enjoy being the center of attention. They are comfortable in large groups and thrive in social situations. Extroverts tend to think out loud and process information by discussing it with others. They are more likely to engage in small talk and enjoy the energy of social gatherings.

In contrast, introverts prefer smaller, more intimate social settings. They value deep and meaningful conversations over small talk. Introverts tend to listen more than they speak and carefully choose their words. They often prefer one-on-one interactions or spending time with a close-knit group of friends. Introverts may find large social gatherings overwhelming and may need breaks to recharge during such events.

1.2.3 Communication Styles: Introverts and Extroverts

Introverts and extroverts also have different communication styles. Extroverts are known for their verbal and expressive nature. They are comfortable sharing their thoughts and feelings openly and enjoy engaging in lively discussions. Extroverts often think and speak simultaneously, processing information externally.

On the other hand, introverts are more reserved and thoughtful in their communication. They tend to think before they speak and prefer to express themselves through writing or carefully chosen words. Introverts may need time to process their thoughts internally before sharing them with others. This reflective nature often leads to insightful and well-thought-out contributions to conversations.

1.2.4 Social Stimulation: Introverts and Extroverts

Introverts and extroverts also differ in their response to social stimulation. Extroverts have a higher threshold for external stimulation and seek out activities that provide sensory input. They enjoy fast-paced environments, loud music, and crowded places. Extroverts are more likely to take risks and seek novelty in their experiences.

In contrast, introverts have a lower threshold for external stimulation and are more sensitive to sensory input. They prefer calm and quiet environments and may feel overwhelmed by excessive noise or stimulation. Introverts often seek out activities that allow them to engage in introspection, such as reading, writing, or pursuing creative hobbies.

1.2.5 Misunderstandings and Stereotypes

Unfortunately, introverts often face misunderstandings and stereotypes due to the dominance of extroverted norms in society. Introverts are sometimes labeled as shy, antisocial, or lacking social skills. However, introversion is not a flaw or a weakness; it is simply a different way of processing and interacting with the world.

It is essential to recognize and appreciate the strengths and unique qualities that introverts bring to the table. Introverts are often excellent listeners, deep thinkers, and creative problem solvers. They have a rich inner world and can offer valuable insights and perspectives.

By understanding the differences between introverts and extroverts, we can foster a more inclusive and accepting society that values and respects the needs and preferences of both personality types. Embracing and celebrating introversion allows individuals to thrive and contribute their unique strengths to the world around them.

1.3 Introvert Traits and Characteristics

Introversion is often misunderstood and misrepresented in society. Many people have misconceptions about what it means to be an introvert, leading to stereotypes and misunderstandings. In this section, we will explore the traits and characteristics commonly associated with introverts, shedding light on the unique qualities that make introverts who they are.

1.3.1 The Need for Solitude

One of the defining traits of introverts is their need for solitude. Introverts often find solace and rejuvenation in spending time alone. Unlike extroverts who gain energy from social interactions, introverts recharge by being in quiet and peaceful environments. This need for solitude is not a sign of being antisocial or unfriendly, but rather a way for introverts to reflect, recharge, and process their thoughts and emotions.

1.3.2 Thoughtfulness and Reflectiveness

Introverts are known for their deep thinking and introspective nature. They tend to be thoughtful and reflective individuals who carefully consider their words and actions. This thoughtfulness often leads to a deeper understanding of themselves and the world around them. Introverts are more likely to engage in introspection, examining their thoughts, feelings, and motivations, which can lead to personal growth and self-awareness.

1.3.3 Listening Skills and Empathy

Introverts are often excellent listeners. They have a natural inclination to listen attentively and empathetically to others. Rather than dominating conversations, introverts prefer to observe and absorb information before sharing their own thoughts. This ability to listen and empathize allows introverts to form deep connections with others and offer valuable support and understanding.

1.3.4 Preference for Meaningful Connections

While introverts may not thrive in large social gatherings, they value deep and meaningful connections. They prefer quality over quantity when it comes to relationships, seeking out individuals with whom they can have profound conversations and share their innermost thoughts and feelings. Introverts appreciate the depth and intimacy that comes with close friendships and romantic relationships.

1.3.5 Sensitivity to Stimuli

Introverts are often more sensitive to external stimuli than extroverts. They may be easily overwhelmed by loud noises, bright lights, or crowded environments. This sensitivity can lead to a preference for calm and quiet surroundings. Introverts may also be more attuned to subtle details and nuances in their environment, which can contribute to their creativity and attention to detail.

1.3.6 Preference for Written Communication

Introverts often find solace in written communication. They may feel more comfortable expressing themselves through writing rather than speaking. Writing allows introverts to carefully choose their words and articulate their thoughts and emotions in a way that feels more natural to them. This preference for written communication can also be seen in their love for reading and consuming information through books and articles.

1.3.7 Independent and Self-Sufficient

Introverts tend to be independent and self-sufficient individuals. They are comfortable being alone and are often capable of entertaining themselves without relying on others for stimulation. This self-sufficiency allows introverts to pursue their interests and hobbies with dedication and focus. They are often content with their own company and can find joy and fulfillment in solitary activities.

1.3.8 Observant and Detail-Oriented

Introverts have a keen sense of observation and are often detail-oriented. They notice things that others may overlook and can pick up on subtle cues and changes in their environment. This attentiveness to detail can be seen in their work, relationships, and creative pursuits. Introverts often excel in tasks that require precision and attention to detail.

1.3.9 Thoughtful Decision-Making

Introverts are known for their thoughtful and deliberate decision-making process. They take the time to weigh the pros and cons, consider different perspectives, and reflect on the potential outcomes before making a decision. This thoughtful approach allows introverts to make well-informed choices and avoid impulsive actions. While this decision-making style may take longer, it often leads to more thoughtful and considered outcomes.

1.3.10 Creativity and Imagination

Introverts often possess a rich inner world filled with creativity and imagination. They have a unique ability to think deeply and explore ideas and concepts in their minds. This imaginative nature often translates into artistic pursuits such as writing, painting, music, or other creative outlets. Introverts can find inspiration and solace in their creative endeavors, allowing them to express themselves in ways that may be challenging through verbal communication.

Understanding the traits and characteristics associated with introverts is crucial in dispelling misconceptions and appreciating the unique qualities that introverts bring to the world. By recognizing and valuing these traits, we can create a more inclusive and understanding society that embraces the diversity of introversion.

1.4 The Power of Introversion

Introversion is often misunderstood and undervalued in a society that celebrates extroversion. Many people mistakenly believe that introverts are shy, anti-social, or lacking in social skills. However, introversion is not a weakness to be overcome, but rather a unique and powerful trait that brings its own set of strengths and advantages.

1.4.1 The Strength of Reflection and Thoughtfulness

One of the greatest powers of introversion lies in the ability to reflect deeply and think critically. Introverts have a natural inclination towards introspection, which allows them to delve into their thoughts and emotions on a profound level. This introspective nature enables introverts to gain a deeper understanding of themselves and the world around them.

By taking the time to reflect and analyze, introverts are able to make well-thought-out decisions and consider multiple perspectives. This thoughtful approach often leads to more insightful and creative solutions to problems. Introverts have the power to see beyond the surface and uncover hidden meanings and connections that others may overlook.

1.4.2 The Power of Listening and Observation

Introverts are known for their exceptional listening skills and keen observation. In social settings, introverts often prefer to listen and observe rather than dominate the conversation. This allows them to pick up on subtle cues, body language, and non-verbal communication that others may miss.

By actively listening and observing, introverts are able to gain a deeper understanding of people and situations. This enables them to form meaningful connections and build strong relationships based on empathy and understanding. The power of observation also extends to the world around them, as introverts often notice details and patterns that others may overlook.

1.4.3 The Strength of Focus and Concentration

Introverts excel in tasks that require deep focus and concentration. They have the ability to block out distractions and immerse themselves fully in their work or hobbies. This allows them to achieve a level of productivity and excellence that is often unmatched.

The power of focus and concentration enables introverts to dive deep into their areas of interest and expertise. They have the ability to become experts in their chosen fields, as they are not easily swayed by external influences or distractions. This strength often leads to innovative ideas, breakthroughs, and significant contributions in various domains.

1.4.4 The Power of Empathy and Emotional Intelligence

Introverts are often highly empathetic and possess a strong sense of emotional intelligence. They have the ability to understand and connect with others on a deep emotional level. This enables them to offer genuine support, guidance, and comfort to those around them.

The power of empathy allows introverts to create safe and nurturing spaces for others. They are often sought after as trusted confidants and advisors due to their ability to listen without judgment and provide thoughtful insights. Introverts have the power to make a positive impact on the lives of those around them through their empathetic nature.

1.4.5 The Strength of Creativity and Innovation

Introverts have a rich inner world that fuels their creativity and imagination. They often find inspiration in solitude and use their introspective nature to explore new ideas and concepts. This allows them to come up with unique and innovative solutions to problems.

The power of creativity and innovation in introverts is often expressed through various forms of art, writing, and other creative outlets. They have the ability to think outside the box and challenge conventional wisdom, leading to groundbreaking discoveries and advancements in various fields.

1.4.6 The Power of Self-Reflection and Growth

Introverts have a natural inclination towards self-reflection and personal growth. They are constantly seeking to understand themselves better and improve in various aspects of their lives. This introspective nature allows them to identify their strengths and weaknesses, and work towards personal development.

The power of self-reflection and growth enables introverts to continuously evolve and become the best version of themselves. They are not afraid to confront their inner demons and address areas that need improvement. This commitment to self-improvement often leads to a deep sense of fulfillment and personal satisfaction.

In conclusion, introversion is not a weakness to be overcome, but a unique and powerful trait that brings its own set of strengths and advantages. The power of introversion lies in the ability to reflect deeply, listen attentively, focus intensely, empathize genuinely, create innovatively, and grow personally. By embracing and harnessing these strengths, introverts can thrive in a world that often misunderstands them and celebrate their unique contributions.

2

Chapter 2

The Introverts Inner World

2.1 The Introvert's Mind

Introverts have a unique way of processing information and experiencing the world around them. Their minds are often a complex labyrinth of thoughts, emotions, and ideas that can be both fascinating and overwhelming. In this section, we will delve into the intricacies of the introvert's mind and explore how it shapes their perception of the world.

2.1.1 The Inner World of Thoughts

The introvert's mind is a bustling hub of thoughts and ideas. Unlike extroverts who tend to process their thoughts externally through conversation and interaction, introverts prefer to internalize their thoughts and reflect upon them in solitude. This internal dialogue allows introverts to deeply analyze and understand their own experiences, leading to a rich inner world of thoughts and ideas.

Introverts often have a vivid imagination and a penchant for daydreaming. Their minds are constantly buzzing with creative ideas, hypothetical scenarios, and deep introspection. This rich inner world is a source of inspiration and solace for introverts, providing them with a sanctuary where they can explore their thoughts and emotions without external distractions.

2.1.2 The Power of Observation

One of the defining characteristics of introverts is their keen observation skills. Introverts have a natural inclination to observe and absorb their surroundings, paying attention to the smallest details that others may overlook. This heightened awareness allows introverts to gain a deeper understanding of the world and the people around them.

Introverts often excel at picking up on subtle cues and non-verbal communication. They are skilled at reading between the lines and understanding the underlying emotions and motivations of others. This ability to observe and analyze helps introverts navigate social interactions with a greater sense of empathy and understanding.

2.1.3 The Need for Reflection

Introverts have a deep need for reflection and introspection. They require ample time alone to process their thoughts and recharge their energy. This need for solitude is not a sign of antisocial behavior or a lack of interest in others; rather, it is a fundamental aspect of their personality that allows them to thrive.

During periods of solitude, introverts engage in deep reflection, analyzing their experiences and emotions. This introspective process helps introverts gain a deeper understanding of themselves and their place in the world. It allows them to recharge their energy and find clarity amidst the noise and chaos of everyday life.

2.1.4 The Complexity of Emotions

Introverts experience emotions deeply and intensely. Their rich inner world often amplifies their emotional experiences, making them more attuned to their own feelings and the emotions of others. This heightened emotional sensitivity can be both a blessing and a challenge for introverts.

Introverts may find themselves easily overwhelmed by intense emotions, requiring time alone to process and regulate their feelings. They may also struggle with expressing their emotions outwardly, preferring to keep them internalized. This can sometimes lead to misunderstandings, as others may misinterpret introverts' reserved nature as a lack of emotional depth or interest.

2.1.5 The Analytical Mind

Introverts have a natural inclination towards analytical thinking. They enjoy delving into complex problems, analyzing different perspectives, and seeking logical solutions. This analytical mindset allows introverts to approach challenges with a methodical and thoughtful approach.

Introverts often excel in fields that require deep analysis and critical thinking, such as science, research, and writing. Their ability to think deeply and consider multiple angles allows them to uncover unique insights and make well-informed decisions. This analytical prowess is a valuable asset that introverts bring to various aspects of their lives.

In conclusion, the introvert's mind is a fascinating and intricate landscape of thoughts, observations, and emotions. Their unique way of processing information and experiencing the world shapes their perception and interactions. Understanding and appreciating the complexities of the introvert's mind can help bridge the gap of misunderstanding and foster greater empathy and acceptance in our extroverted-centric society.

2.2 Introvert's Need for Solitude

Introverts have a unique and deep need for solitude. It is an essential aspect of their personality and plays a crucial role in their overall well-being. While extroverts thrive in social interactions and gain energy from being around others, introverts find solace and recharge their energy through spending time alone.

The Power of Solitude

Solitude is not synonymous with loneliness or isolation. It is a conscious choice to be alone and engage in activities that bring inner peace and fulfillment. For introverts, solitude is a sanctuary where they can retreat from the noise and demands of the external world. It provides them with the opportunity to reflect, recharge, and reconnect with themselves on a deeper level.

Understanding the Introvert's Perspective

To truly grasp the significance of solitude for introverts, it is essential to understand their perspective. Introverts process information internally, and their thoughts and ideas flourish in the quietness of their own minds. They often have a rich inner world that is fueled by introspection, reflection, and deep thinking. Solitude allows them the space and freedom to explore their thoughts, emotions, and creativity without external distractions.

Recharging Energy

One of the primary reasons introverts seek solitude is to recharge their energy. Social interactions, especially in large groups or for extended periods, can be draining for introverts. They require time alone to replenish their energy reserves and regain their mental and emotional balance. Solitude provides them with the opportunity to rest, rejuvenate, and regain their sense of self.

Self-Reflection and Introspection

Solitude offers introverts the chance to engage in self-reflection and introspection. They are naturally inclined to analyze their thoughts, feelings, and experiences. Through introspection, introverts gain a deeper understanding of themselves, their values, and their goals. They use this time alone to explore their innermost thoughts, process their emotions, and make sense of the world around them.

Cultivating Creativity and Imagination

Introverts often possess a rich imagination and a deep well of creativity. Solitude allows them to tap into this creativity and explore their ideas without external distractions or interruptions. In the quietness of solitude, introverts can fully immerse themselves in their creative pursuits, whether it be writing, painting, or any other form of artistic expression. They can let their imagination run wild and bring their unique visions to life.

Finding Peace and Serenity

Solitude provides introverts with a sense of peace and serenity. It is in these moments of solitude that they can find solace from the overwhelming noise and stimulation of the outside world. Introverts appreciate the tranquility that solitude brings, allowing them to find inner peace and recharge their spirits. It is during these moments that they can truly be themselves, free from the pressures of conforming to societal expectations.

Balancing Solitude and Social Interaction

While solitude is essential for introverts, it is important to note that they still value meaningful social interactions. Introverts may prefer smaller, intimate gatherings or one-on-one conversations rather than large social events. They appreciate deep connections and meaningful conversations that allow them to engage on a more profound level. It is about finding a balance between solitude and social interaction that works best for each individual introvert.

Respecting the Introvert's Need for Solitude

It is crucial for both introverts and those around them to respect their need for solitude. Introverts should not feel guilty or pressured to constantly engage in social activities if it drains their energy. Instead, they should embrace and prioritize their need for solitude as a means of self-care and personal growth. Likewise, those in the lives of introverts should understand and support their need for alone time, recognizing that it is not a reflection of their disinterest or lack of affection.

Conclusion

The need for solitude is an integral part of the introvert's identity. It is through solitude that introverts find solace, recharge their energy, and cultivate their creativity. Understanding and respecting this need is essential for introverts to thrive and for others to appreciate the unique qualities introverts bring to the world. Solitude is not a weakness but a source of strength and self-discovery for introverts, allowing them to navigate the world in their own authentic way.

2.3 Introvert's Reflection and Introspection

Introverts have a unique way of processing information and interacting with the world around them. While extroverts tend to thrive in social situations and gain energy from being around others, introverts often find solace and rejuvenation in solitude. This preference for introspection and reflection is a defining characteristic of introversion.

The Power of Reflection

Introverts have a natural inclination towards introspection, which involves deep self-reflection and examination of one's thoughts, feelings, and experiences. This process allows introverts to gain a deeper understanding of themselves and the world around them. By taking the time to reflect, introverts can make sense of their emotions, motivations, and desires, leading to personal growth and self-awareness.

Reflection provides introverts with the opportunity to process their experiences and make meaning out of them. It allows them to analyze their thoughts and actions, identify patterns, and gain insights into their own behavior. This self-reflection helps introverts make informed decisions and navigate their lives with a greater sense of purpose and clarity.

The Importance of Solitude

Introverts often seek solitude as a means of recharging and rejuvenating themselves. It is during these moments of solitude that introverts engage in deep reflection and introspection. Solitude provides introverts with the space and freedom to explore their inner thoughts and emotions without external distractions.

In a world that often values constant social interaction and stimulation, introverts may face challenges in finding the necessary time and space for solitude. However, it is crucial for introverts to prioritize and carve out moments of solitude in their lives. This dedicated time for reflection allows introverts to recharge their energy, process their thoughts, and gain a deeper understanding of themselves.

The Gift of Introspection

Introverts possess a unique gift for introspection, which allows them to delve into the depths of their own minds and explore their inner worlds. This introspective nature enables introverts to develop a rich inner life filled with thoughts, ideas, and imaginings. It is through this introspection that introverts often find inspiration and creativity.

Introspection allows introverts to tap into their inner resources and explore their thoughts and emotions in a profound way. It is during these moments of deep introspection that introverts can uncover hidden insights, generate new ideas, and make connections that others may overlook. This ability to dive deep into their own minds gives introverts a unique perspective and allows them to approach problems and challenges from a fresh and innovative angle.

Cultivating Introspection

While introverts naturally possess a propensity for introspection, it is a skill that can be further developed and cultivated. Here are a few strategies that introverts can employ to enhance their introspective abilities:

1. Create dedicated introspection time: Set aside specific periods in your day or week for introspection. Find a quiet and comfortable space where you can be alone with your thoughts and engage in deep reflection.

2. Journaling: Writing down your thoughts and feelings in a journal can be a powerful tool for introspection. It allows you to externalize your thoughts and gain a clearer understanding of your inner world.

3. Mindfulness and meditation: Practicing mindfulness and meditation can help introverts cultivate a sense of presence and awareness. These practices encourage introspection by allowing you to observe your thoughts and emotions without judgment.

4. Engage in creative activities: Activities such as painting, writing, or playing a musical instrument can stimulate introspection and unlock your creative potential. These creative outlets provide a space for self-expression and exploration.

5. Seek solitude in nature: Spending time in nature can be incredibly rejuvenating for introverts. The peacefulness and beauty of the natural world can inspire deep introspection and reflection.

By incorporating these practices into their lives, introverts can further harness the power of introspection and deepen their understanding of themselves and the world around them.

In conclusion, introverts possess a unique ability for reflection and introspection. This gift allows them to gain self-awareness, make meaning out of their experiences, and tap into their creative potential. By embracing and cultivating their introspective nature, introverts can navigate the world with a greater sense of purpose and authenticity.

2.4 Introvert's Creativity and Imagination

Introverts possess a unique and powerful gift: their creativity and imagination. While extroverts may thrive in social interactions and external stimulation, introverts find solace and inspiration within their own minds. This chapter explores the rich inner world of introverts and how their creativity and imagination shape their lives.

2.4.1 The Creative Mind of an Introvert

Introverts have a natural inclination towards creativity. Their ability to spend time alone and reflect allows them to tap into their inner thoughts and emotions, which often leads to innovative and imaginative ideas. The quiet and introspective nature of introverts provides them with the mental space needed to explore new concepts and perspectives.

In the realm of creativity, introverts often excel in various artistic endeavors. Whether it be painting, writing, music, or any other form of artistic expression, introverts have a unique ability to channel their thoughts and emotions into their creative work. Their deep introspection allows them to create pieces that are not only aesthetically pleasing but also deeply meaningful.

2.4.2 Imagination: The Playground of Introverts

Introverts possess a vivid and expansive imagination. Their ability to daydream and create intricate mental landscapes is unparalleled. While extroverts may seek external stimulation, introverts find endless fascination within their own minds. This imaginative playground serves as a source of inspiration and solace for introverts.

Through their imagination, introverts can explore different scenarios, envision future possibilities, and delve into the depths of their own desires and fears. This rich inner world fuels their creativity and allows them to bring their ideas to life. Whether it be through storytelling, problem-solving, or envisioning new concepts, introverts' imagination is a powerful tool that sets them apart.

2.4.3 The Power of Solitude in Fostering Creativity

Solitude is the breeding ground for introverts' creativity and imagination. It is during these moments of quiet introspection that introverts can fully immerse themselves in their thoughts and ideas. The absence of external distractions allows them to focus deeply on their creative pursuits.

Unlike extroverts who may draw inspiration from social interactions, introverts find their muse in solitude. It is in these moments of stillness that their minds wander freely, connecting seemingly unrelated ideas and concepts. This ability to make unique connections and think deeply about their creative endeavors is what sets introverts apart in the realm of creativity.

2.4.4 Embracing the Introvert's Creative Process

The creative process of an introvert is often different from that of an extrovert. While extroverts may thrive in collaborative and fast-paced environments, introverts require a more introspective and deliberate approach. They need time to process their thoughts and ideas before sharing them with others.

Introverts may prefer to work alone, allowing them to fully immerse themselves in their creative process without external distractions. They may find solace in quiet spaces, where they can let their imagination run wild and explore new possibilities. This preference for solitude should not be seen as a limitation but rather as a strength that allows introverts to produce their best work.

2.4.5 Nurturing and Supporting Introverts' Creativity

To nurture and support introverts' creativity, it is essential to create an environment that values and respects their need for solitude and introspection. Providing them with dedicated spaces where they can retreat and focus on their creative pursuits is crucial. Additionally, allowing them the freedom to work at their own pace and providing opportunities for deep reflection can greatly enhance their creative output.

Collaboration can also be beneficial for introverts, but it should be approached in a way that respects their need for solitude. Offering them the option to contribute their ideas in writing or through one-on-one discussions can help introverts feel more comfortable and valued in collaborative settings.

2.4.6 The Unique Contributions of Introverts' Creativity

Introverts' creativity and imagination bring a unique perspective to the world. Their ability to think deeply, make connections, and explore the depths of their own minds allows them to offer fresh and innovative ideas. Their creative works often reflect their introspective nature, providing a glimpse into their rich inner world.

In various fields, introverts have made significant contributions through their creativity. From literature to art, from scientific discoveries to technological advancements, introverts have left an indelible mark on society. Their ability to see beyond the surface and delve into the complexities of life allows them to create works that resonate deeply with others.

2.4.7 Embracing and Celebrating Introverts' Creativity

It is essential for society to recognize and celebrate the creativity of introverts. By understanding and appreciating their unique approach to creativity, we can create an inclusive environment that values the contributions of introverts. This recognition can help introverts feel empowered and confident in expressing their creative ideas.

As individuals, introverts can embrace their creativity by honoring their need for solitude and introspection. By creating a routine that allows for regular periods of reflection and creative exploration, introverts can tap into their full creative potential. Embracing their unique perspective and finding joy in their creative process can lead to a fulfilling and meaningful creative journey.

In conclusion, introverts possess a remarkable gift in their creativity and imagination. Their ability to tap into their inner thoughts and emotions, their vivid imagination, and their need for solitude all contribute to their unique approach to creativity. By understanding and supporting introverts' creative process, we can create a world that celebrates and embraces the valuable contributions of introverts.

3

Chapter 3

Navigating Social Interactions

3.1 Introverts and Small Talk

Small talk is a common social interaction that many people engage in on a daily basis. It involves casual conversations about general topics such as the weather, current events, or weekend plans. While small talk may seem harmless and effortless for some, it can be a source of discomfort and anxiety for introverts.

Introverts are individuals who gain energy from spending time alone and often prefer deep, meaningful conversations over superficial chit-chat. They tend to be more introspective and thoughtful, which can make engaging in small talk challenging. The nature of small talk, with its focus on surface-level topics and quick exchanges, can leave introverts feeling drained and disconnected.

For introverts, small talk can feel like a social obligation rather than a genuine form of communication. They may struggle to find the right words or feel pressured to keep the conversation going. This can lead to feelings of anxiety and self-consciousness, as introverts may worry about being judged or misunderstood.

One of the reasons why introverts find small talk challenging is that it often lacks depth and authenticity. Introverts thrive on meaningful connections and conversations that allow them to explore ideas and emotions on a deeper level. Small talk, with its emphasis on superficial topics, can feel shallow and unfulfilling to introverts.

Additionally, introverts tend to be more introspective and reflective, which means they may need more time to process their thoughts before responding in a conversation. This can make small talk feel overwhelming, as introverts may feel pressured to come up with quick and witty responses on the spot.

Another aspect of small talk that introverts struggle with is the need to constantly engage in social interactions. Introverts value their alone time and often need periods of solitude to recharge and reflect. Small talk, with its constant demand for social engagement, can leave introverts feeling drained and overwhelmed.

It is important to note that introverts are not anti-social or lacking social skills. They simply have a different preference when it comes to social interactions. Introverts often excel in one-on-one conversations or in small groups where they can engage in more meaningful discussions. They may prefer to listen and observe rather than dominate the conversation.

Understanding and respecting the introvert's need for deeper connections can help create a more inclusive and supportive social environment. Instead of pressuring introverts to engage in small talk, it is important to provide opportunities for more meaningful conversations. This can be done by asking open-ended questions that encourage introspection and sharing personal experiences.

For introverts who find small talk challenging, there are strategies that can help navigate these situations. One approach is to focus on finding common interests or topics that genuinely interest the introvert. By steering the conversation towards subjects that they are passionate about, introverts can feel more engaged and comfortable.

Another strategy is to practice active listening. Introverts are often skilled listeners and can use this strength to their advantage in small talk situations. By actively listening and showing genuine interest in the other person's perspective, introverts can create a more meaningful connection even in superficial conversations.

It is also important for introverts to set boundaries and prioritize self-care. Recognizing when they need time alone to recharge and taking breaks from social interactions can help introverts maintain their energy and well-being. By understanding and respecting their own needs, introverts can navigate small talk with more confidence and ease.

In conclusion, small talk can be a challenging aspect of social interactions for introverts. The superficial nature of small talk and the constant demand for social engagement can leave introverts feeling drained and disconnected. However, by understanding and respecting the introvert's need for deeper connections, providing opportunities for meaningful conver-sations, and practicing strategies such as focusing on common interests and active listening, introverts can navigate small talk with more confidence and ease.

3.2 Introverts in Group Settings

Introverts often find themselves in group settings, whether it be at work, social gatherings, or even within their own families. These situations can be challenging for introverts, as they may feel overwhelmed by the constant stimulation and pressure to engage with others. In this section, we will explore the unique experiences and dilemmas that introverts face in group settings and discuss strategies for navigating these situations.

3.2.1 The Introvert's Dilemma

For introverts, group settings can be both exhausting and anxiety-inducing. The constant noise, chatter, and social expectations can drain their energy and leave them feeling overwhelmed. Unlike extroverts who thrive in social environments, introverts need time alone to recharge and process their thoughts and emotions. This need for solitude can often clash with the demands of group settings, where constant interaction and engagement are expected.

3.2.2 The Pressure to Conform

In group settings, introverts may feel pressured to conform to extroverted norms and behaviors. They may be expected to participate in group discussions, speak up, and assert themselves in ways that may not come naturally to them. This pressure to conform can be particularly challenging for introverts, as it goes against their preference for reflection and thoughtful communication. As a result, introverts may feel misunderstood or undervalued in group settings.

3.2.3 The Art of Observation

While introverts may not be the most vocal participants in group settings, they often excel in observation. Introverts have a keen ability to listen and observe, which allows them to gain valuable insights and perspectives. By taking a step back and observing the dynamics of the group, introverts can contribute in meaningful ways by offering thoughtful and well-considered input. This ability to observe and analyze can be a valuable asset in group settings, where different perspectives are needed for effective decision-making.

3.2.4 Finding Balance

Finding a balance between participating in group settings and honoring one's introverted nature can be a delicate dance for introverts. It is important for introverts to recognize and respect their need for solitude and recharge time, while also finding ways to engage and contribute in group settings. This may involve setting boundaries, such as taking breaks during social events or finding quiet spaces to retreat to when needed. By finding this balance, introverts can navigate group settings more comfortably and authentically.

3.2.5 Harnessing the Power of Preparation

One strategy that introverts can employ in group settings is the power of preparation. Introverts often thrive when they have time to gather their thoughts and prepare for social interactions. By taking the time to research and gather information before group meetings or events, introverts can feel more confident and prepared to contribute. This preparation can also help introverts overcome any anxiety or self-doubt they may experience in group settings.

3.2.6 Building Meaningful Connections

While introverts may prefer deeper and more meaningful connections, group settings can sometimes feel superficial and overwhelming. However, it is still possible for introverts to build meaningful connections within these settings. By seeking out smaller, more intimate conversations within the larger group, introverts can engage in deeper discussions and connect with others on a more personal level. Additionally, introverts can focus on building connections with like-minded individuals who understand and appreciate their introverted nature.

3.2.7 Self-Care in Group Settings

Taking care of oneself in group settings is crucial for introverts. It is important for introverts to prioritize self-care and recognize when they need to step away and recharge. This may involve finding moments of solitude during group events, engaging in activities that bring them joy and relaxation, or simply taking breaks to recharge their energy. By practicing self-care in group settings, introverts can better manage their energy levels and prevent burnout.

3.2.8 Communicating Needs and Boundaries

Open and honest communication is key for introverts in group settings. It is important for introverts to communicate their needs and boundaries to others, so that they can be respected and understood. This may involve expressing the need for alone time, setting limits on social engagements, or explaining their preference for deeper conversations. By communicating their needs and boundaries, introverts can create a more supportive and understanding environment within group settings.

3.2.9 Embracing the Introvert's Unique Perspective

Introverts bring a unique perspective to group settings. Their ability to listen, observe, and reflect can offer valuable insights and contribute to more well-rounded discussions. It is important for introverts to embrace and value their unique perspective, even if it may differ from the more extroverted voices in the group. By embracing their introverted nature and the strengths it brings, introverts can navigate group settings with confidence and authenticity.

In conclusion, group settings can present challenges for introverts, but with self-awareness, preparation, and effective communication, introverts can navigate these situations successfully. By finding a balance between solitude and engagement, introverts can contribute their unique perspectives and build meaningful connections within group settings. It is important for introverts to embrace their introverted nature and recognize the strengths it brings to group dynamics.

3.3 Introverts and Networking

Networking can be a daunting task for introverts. The thought of engaging in small talk, meeting new people, and making connections can be overwhelming. Introverts often find themselves in situations where they feel misunderstood and out of place. This section will explore the challenges introverts face when it comes to networking and provide strategies to navigate these situations with confidence.

3.3.1 The Introvert's Perspective

Introverts are often misunderstood in social settings, and networking is no exception. While extroverts thrive in social interactions and gain energy from being around others, introverts tend to feel drained by excessive socializing. This fundamental difference in energy sources can make networking events particularly challenging for introverts.

Introverts prefer deep and meaningful conversations over small talk. They value quality connections over quantity. This preference can make it difficult for introverts to engage in superficial conversations that are often a part of networking events. Introverts may feel pressured to conform to societal expectations of being outgoing and talkative, which can lead to feelings of anxiety and discomfort.

3.3.2 Embracing Your Introversion

The first step in navigating networking events as an introvert is to embrace your introversion. Recognize that being introverted is not a flaw or a weakness but a unique personality trait. Understand that introverts have their own strengths and qualities that can be valuable in networking situations.

Instead of trying to mimic extroverted behavior, focus on leveraging your introverted strengths. Introverts are often great listeners and observers, which can be advantageous in networking. By actively listening and paying attention to others, introverts can make meaningful connections and engage in more substantial conversations.

3.3.3 Preparation is Key

For introverts, preparation is key when it comes to networking. Before attending an event, take some time to research the attendees, speakers, or topics that will be discussed. Having some background knowledge can help introverts feel more confident and prepared for conversations.

Additionally, consider setting specific goals for the networking event. Instead of trying to meet as many people as possible, focus on connecting with a few individuals who share similar interests or goals. This targeted approach can help introverts feel more comfortable and make the networking experience more meaningful.

3.3.4 Finding Common Ground

One effective strategy for introverts in networking situations is to find common ground with others. Look for shared interests, hobbies, or experiences that can serve as conversation starters. By focusing on commonalities, introverts can establish a genuine connection and engage in more meaningful conversations.

Introverts can also use their natural curiosity to their advantage. Asking open-ended questions and showing genuine interest in others can help introverts build rapport and create a comfortable atmosphere. This approach allows introverts to take the spotlight off themselves and focus on the other person, alleviating some of the pressure they may feel in networking situations.

3.3.5 Taking Breaks and Recharging

Networking events can be overwhelming for introverts, as they often involve large crowds and continuous social interactions. It is essential for introverts to recognize their limits and take breaks when needed. Find a quiet corner or step outside for a few minutes to recharge and gather your thoughts.

Introverts may also benefit from setting boundaries during networking events. It is okay to decline invitations to after-parties or social gatherings if you feel overwhelmed. Prioritizing self-care and honoring your need for solitude is crucial for introverts to maintain their energy and well-being.

3.3.6 Building a Supportive Network

Networking doesn't have to be a solo endeavor for introverts. Building a supportive network of like-minded individuals can provide introverts with a sense of belonging and support. Seek out networking groups or communities that cater to introverts or individuals with similar interests.

By connecting with others who understand and appreciate introversion, introverts can find a safe space to share experiences, exchange advice, and build meaningful relationships. These supportive networks can also serve as a platform for introverts to practice their networking skills in a more comfortable and understanding environment.

3.3.7 Seeking Professional Development Opportunities

Networking is not just about making connections; it is also an opportunity for professional growth. Introverts can leverage networking events to expand their knowledge, gain insights from industry experts, and stay updated on the latest trends in their field.

Consider attending workshops, seminars, or conferences that align with your professional interests. These events often provide structured networking opportunities, such as panel discussions or breakout sessions, which can be less overwhelming for introverts. By focusing on the learning aspect of networking events, introverts can shift their mindset and approach these situations with a sense of purpose and enthusiasm.

3.3.8 Practice Makes Perfect

Like any skill, networking requires practice. Introverts may initially find networking events challenging, but with time and experience, they can become more comfortable and confident in these settings. Start by attending smaller, more intimate networking events or practice networking in a one-on-one setting with a mentor or colleague.

Remember that networking is not about being the loudest or most outgoing person in the room. It is about building genuine connections, sharing knowledge, and supporting one another. By embracing your introversion and leveraging your unique strengths, you can navigate networking events with authenticity and success.

3.3.9 Conclusion

Networking as an introvert may seem like a daunting task, but with the right mindset and strategies, it can become a rewarding experience. Embrace your introversion, prepare in advance, find common ground, take breaks when needed, and build a supportive network. Remember that networking is not about changing who you are but about leveraging your strengths and making meaningful connections. By embracing your introversion and navigating networking events with confidence, you can create opportunities for personal and professional growth.

3.4 Introverts and Public Speaking

Public speaking is often considered one of the most anxiety-inducing activities for introverts. The thought of standing in front of a large audience, being the center of attention, and delivering a speech can be overwhelming for those who thrive in quieter, more introspective settings. However, it is important to recognize that introverts can excel in public speaking and make a powerful impact when given the opportunity to share their thoughts and ideas.

The Fear of Public Speaking

For many introverts, the fear of public speaking stems from a variety of factors. One of the main reasons is the fear of judgment and scrutiny from others. Introverts tend to be more self-conscious and may worry about making mistakes or being perceived negatively by the audience. The pressure to perform and meet the expectations of others can be daunting, leading to anxiety and nervousness.

Another aspect that contributes to the fear of public speaking is the energy drain that comes from being in a highly stimulating environment. Introverts thrive in quieter, more controlled settings where they can reflect and recharge. The thought of being in the spotlight and having to engage with a large group of people for an extended period can be mentally and emotionally exhausting for introverts.

Overcoming the Fear

While public speaking may not come naturally to introverts, it is a skill that can be developed and mastered with practice and the right mindset. Here are some strategies that can help introverts overcome their fear of public speaking:

1. Preparation is Key

Introverts tend to excel in tasks that require careful planning and preparation. Before giving a speech, take the time to thoroughly research and organize your thoughts. Create a well-structured outline and practice your speech multiple times. The more familiar you are with the content, the more confident you will feel when delivering it.

2. Start Small

Instead of diving into a large-scale public speaking event right away, start by speaking in smaller, more intimate settings. This could include presenting in front of a small group of friends or colleagues, joining a public speaking club, or participating in workshops or seminars. Gradually increasing the size of the audience will help build confidence and reduce anxiety.

3. Focus on the Message

Instead of fixating on your own performance or worrying about how you are being perceived, shift your focus to the message you want to convey. Remember that the audience is there to listen to what you have to say and learn from your expertise. By focusing on the value you can provide to others, you can redirect your energy away from self-doubt and towards delivering a meaningful presentation.

4. Utilize Introvert Strengths

Introverts possess unique strengths that can be leveraged in public speaking. Their ability to listen attentively, think deeply, and communicate thoughtfully can captivate an audience. Use these strengths to your advantage by incorporating storytelling, engaging visuals, and well-researched content into your speech. By playing to your strengths, you can create a memorable and impactful presentation.

5. Practice Mindfulness and Self-Care

Prioritize self-care and practice mindfulness techniques to manage anxiety and stress associated with public speaking. Engage in activities that help you relax and recharge, such as meditation, deep breathing exercises, or engaging in hobbies that bring you joy. Taking care of your mental and emotional well-being will contribute to a more confident and composed demeanor when speaking in public.

Embracing Your Unique Voice

It is important for introverts to recognize that their unique perspective and voice have value in the realm of public speaking. While extroverts may thrive in the spotlight, introverts bring a depth of thought and introspection that can resonate with audiences in a profound way. By embracing their introversion and leveraging their strengths, introverts can make a significant impact through public speaking.

Remember, public speaking is a skill that can be developed and refined over time. With practice, preparation, and a positive mindset, introverts can overcome their fear and become powerful communicators. So, the next time you find yourself faced with the opportunity to speak in public, embrace the challenge, and let your unique voice be heard.

3.5 Introverts and Social Anxiety

Social anxiety is a common challenge that many introverts face. While introversion and social anxiety are not the same thing, they can often go hand in hand. Social anxiety is a specific type of anxiety disorder that is characterized by an intense fear of social situations. It can make social interactions incredibly difficult and overwhelming for those who experience it.

For introverts, who already tend to prefer solitude and quiet environments, social anxiety can be particularly challenging. The fear of judgment, embarrassment, or being the center of attention can make social situations feel incredibly uncomfortable and anxiety-inducing. This can lead to a reluctance to engage in social activities, avoiding social gatherings, and even isolating oneself from others.

One of the reasons why introverts may be more prone to social anxiety is because they often feel misunderstood or judged by others. Society tends to value extroverted qualities such as being outgoing, talkative, and assertive, while introverts are often seen as shy, reserved, or even anti-social. This misunderstanding can create a sense of pressure for introverts to conform to extroverted norms, which can exacerbate social anxiety.

Another factor that contributes to social anxiety in introverts is the tendency to overthink and analyze social interactions. Introverts are known for their introspective nature and their tendency to reflect deeply on their thoughts and feelings. This can lead to a heightened self-awareness and self-consciousness in social situations, as introverts may constantly worry about how they are perceived by others.

It is important to note that not all introverts experience social anxiety, and not all individuals with social anxiety are introverts. However, the overlap between introversion and social anxiety is significant, and it is crucial to understand and address the unique challenges that introverts with social anxiety face.

So, how can introverts with social anxiety navigate social interactions and manage their anxiety? Here are some strategies that can be helpful:

3.5.1 Understanding and Accepting Social Anxiety

The first step in managing social anxiety is to understand and accept it. Recognize that social anxiety is a common challenge and that you are not alone in experiencing it. It is not a character flaw or a weakness, but rather a natural response to certain situations. By acknowledging and accepting your social anxiety, you can begin to develop strategies to cope with it.

3.5.2 Gradual Exposure and Desensitization

One effective approach to managing social anxiety is gradual exposure and desensitization. Start by exposing yourself to small, manageable social situations that make you slightly uncomfortable. As you become more comfortable, gradually increase the level of exposure. This gradual approach allows you to build confidence and reduce anxiety over time.

3.5.3 Developing Coping Mechanisms

Identify and develop coping mechanisms that work for you. This could include deep breathing exercises, positive self-talk, or visualization techniques. Find strategies that help you relax and manage your anxiety in social situations. It may also be helpful to seek professional help, such as therapy or counseling, to learn additional coping skills.

3.5.4 Setting Realistic Expectations

It is important to set realistic expectations for yourself in social situations. Understand that it is okay to feel nervous or uncomfortable, and that you do not have to be the life of the party. Focus on connecting with others on a deeper level, rather than trying to meet extroverted standards. Remember that introversion is a unique and valuable trait, and that you have strengths to offer in social interactions.

3.5.5 Building a Supportive Network

Surround yourself with understanding and supportive individuals who appreciate and respect your introverted nature. Seek out like-minded individuals who understand your need for solitude and who can provide a safe and comfortable social environment. Building a supportive network can help alleviate social anxiety and create meaningful connections.

3.5.6 Practicing Self-Care

Taking care of yourself is crucial when managing social anxiety. Prioritize self-care activities that help you recharge and reduce stress. This could include engaging in hobbies, spending time alone, or practicing mindfulness and relaxation techniques. By prioritizing self-care, you can better manage your social anxiety and maintain a healthy balance in your life.

Remember, social anxiety is a challenge that many introverts face, but it does not define who you are. By understanding and accepting your social anxiety, developing coping mechanisms, and building a supportive network, you can navigate social interactions with greater ease and confidence. Embrace your introverted nature and celebrate the unique strengths that it brings.

4

Chapter 4

The Introverts Relationships

4.1 Introverts in Romantic Relationships

Introverts often face unique challenges when it comes to romantic relationships. Their need for solitude and preference for deep connections can sometimes be misunderstood by their partners, leading to feelings of frustration and isolation. In this section, we will explore the dynamics of introverts in romantic relationships and provide insights on how to navigate these challenges.

4.1.1 Understanding Introvert-Extrovert Dynamics

One of the most common misunderstandings in introvert-extrovert relationships is the difference in social needs. Extroverts tend to thrive in social settings and gain energy from being around others, while introverts recharge by spending time alone or with a small group of close friends. This fundamental difference can create tension if not properly understood and addressed.

It is crucial for both partners to recognize and respect each other's needs. Introverts should communicate their need for alone time without feeling guilty or judged, while extroverts should understand that it is not a reflection of their partner's lack of interest or love. Open and honest communication is key to finding a balance that works for both individuals.

4.1.2 The Importance of Quality Time

Introverts value deep connections and meaningful conversations. They often prefer spending quality time with their partners rather than engaging in large social gatherings or superficial activities. This can sometimes be challenging for extroverted partners who thrive on constant social interaction.

To foster a healthy relationship, it is important for both partners to find a middle ground. Introverts can make an effort to engage in social activities that their extroverted partners enjoy, while extroverts can create space for intimate one-on-one time where deep conversations can take place. By understanding and appreciating each other's preferences, introverts and extroverts can create a strong foundation for their relationship.

4.1.3 Communication Styles and Conflict Resolution

Introverts often prefer to think before they speak and may need time to process their thoughts and emotions. This can sometimes be misinterpreted as disinterest or lack of engagement by their partners. It is important for introverts to communicate their need for processing time and for their partners to be patient and understanding.

In times of conflict, introverts may need space and time alone to reflect and recharge. It is crucial for both partners to respect this need and find alternative ways to communicate and resolve conflicts. Written communication, such as letters or emails, can be helpful for introverts to express their thoughts and feelings without feeling overwhelmed.

4.1.4 Building Trust and Emotional Intimacy

Introverts tend to value deep emotional connections and may take longer to open up and trust their partners. It is important for their partners to be patient and understanding during this process. Building trust requires consistent support, understanding, and respect for each other's boundaries.

Creating a safe and non-judgmental space for emotional expression is essential for introverts to feel comfortable in a romantic relationship. Partners can encourage open communication by actively listening, validating feelings, and showing empathy. By fostering emotional intimacy, introverts can feel secure and valued in their relationships.

4.1.5 Balancing Independence and Togetherness

Introverts often cherish their independence and may need regular alone time to recharge. This can sometimes be misinterpreted as a lack of interest or commitment by their partners. It is important for introverts to communicate their need for solitude and for their partners to understand that it is not a reflection of their love or desire for the relationship.

Finding a balance between independence and togetherness is crucial in introvert-extrovert relationships. Partners can create a schedule or establish boundaries that allow for both individual and shared activities. This way, introverts can have the space they need while still maintaining a strong connection with their partners.

4.1.6 Embracing and Celebrating Differences

Introvert-extrovert relationships can be incredibly rewarding when both partners embrace and celebrate their differences. By recognizing and appreciating each other's unique qualities, introverts and extroverts can learn from one another and grow together.

It is important for both partners to have a sense of self-awareness and self-acceptance. Introverts should embrace their introversion and communicate their needs, while extroverts should appreciate and respect their partner's need for solitude and reflection.

In conclusion, introverts in romantic relationships face unique challenges that can be overcome with understanding, communication, and mutual respect. By recognizing and appreciating each other's differences, introverts and their partners can build strong and fulfilling relationships that honor their individual needs and preferences.

4.2 Introverts and Friendships

Friendships play a crucial role in our lives, providing companionship, support, and a sense of belonging. For introverts, navigating friendships can be both rewarding and challenging. While introverts may have fewer friends compared to their extroverted counterparts, the depth and quality of their friendships are often unparalleled. In this section, we will explore the unique dynamics of introverts in friendships and shed light on the misconceptions that surround them.

4.2.1 The Introvert's Approach to Friendships

Introverts approach friendships with a thoughtful and intentional mindset. They value deep connections and meaningful conversations over superficial interactions. Unlike extroverts who thrive in large social gatherings, introverts prefer one-on-one or small group settings where they can engage in more intimate conversations. This preference allows introverts to truly connect with their friends on a deeper level, fostering a sense of trust and understanding.

4.2.2 The Misunderstanding of Introversion in Friendships

Unfortunately, introverts often face misunderstandings and misconceptions when it comes to their friendships. Society tends to view introversion as a flaw or a limitation, leading to the belief that introverts are lonely, antisocial, or lacking in social skills. These misconceptions can create barriers in forming and maintaining friendships, as others may not fully understand or appreciate the unique qualities that introverts bring to the table.

4.2.3 Quality over Quantity

One common misconception is that introverts are not interested in making friends or that they are incapable of forming deep connections. This couldn't be further from the truth. While introverts may have a smaller circle of friends, the friendships they do cultivate are often characterized by loyalty, trust, and mutual understanding. Introverts prioritize quality over quantity, investing their time and energy into a select few individuals who truly understand and appreciate them.

4.2.4 The Importance of Alone Time

Another misconception is that introverts are always available and ready to socialize. In reality, introverts require ample alone time to recharge and rejuvenate. This need for solitude should not be mistaken for disinterest or rejection. Introverts value their alone time as an opportunity to reflect, recharge, and process their thoughts and emotions. Understanding and respecting an introvert's need for solitude is crucial in maintaining a healthy and balanced friendship.

4.2.5 Communication and Understanding

Effective communication is key in any friendship, but it holds even greater significance for introverts. Introverts often need time to process their thoughts before expressing them verbally. They may prefer written communication or thoughtful conversations that allow them to fully articulate their ideas. Friends of introverts should be patient and understanding, giving them the space and time they need to express themselves fully.

4.2.6 Mutual Respect and Acceptance

Friendships thrive when there is mutual respect and acceptance. Introverts should not feel pressured to conform to extroverted norms or change their natural tendencies to fit in. True friends will appreciate and embrace the introvert's unique qualities, understanding that introversion is not a flaw but a valuable aspect of their personality. Similarly, introverts should also respect their friends' extroverted nature and provide them with the social stimulation they need.

4.2.7 Nurturing Friendships

Introverts may find it challenging to initiate and maintain friendships, but with a little effort and understanding, they can cultivate meaningful connections. It is important for introverts to step out of their comfort zones occasionally, attending social events or engaging in activities that align with their interests. By doing so, they can meet like-minded individuals and potentially form lasting friendships.

4.2.8 Embracing Diversity in Friendships

Introverts can benefit greatly from having friends who possess different personality traits and perspectives. These diverse friendships can provide new insights, broaden their horizons, and challenge their own beliefs and assumptions. By embracing diversity in friendships, introverts can continue to grow and learn from the experiences and perspectives of others.

4.2.9 The Power of Introverted Friendships

Introverted friendships have a unique power to provide a safe space for introverts to be themselves fully. In these friendships, introverts can feel understood, accepted, and appreciated for who they are. The deep connections and meaningful conversations that introverts share with their friends can be a source of comfort, support, and personal growth.

In conclusion, introverts approach friendships with a thoughtful and intentional mindset, valuing quality over quantity. Misunderstandings and misconceptions surrounding introversion can create barriers in forming and maintaining friendships, but with effective communication, mutual respect, and acceptance, introverts can cultivate meaningful connections that enrich their lives. Embracing diversity in friendships and recognizing the power of introverted friendships can lead to a fulfilling and supportive social network for introverts.

4.3 Introverts and Family Dynamics

Introverts often face unique challenges when it comes to navigating family dynamics. In a world that often values extroversion and social interaction, introverts may find themselves feeling misunderstood and out of place within their own families. This section will explore some of the common issues introverts face in their family relationships and provide strategies for fostering understanding and harmony.

4.3.1 The Introvert's Need for Solitude

One of the key aspects of introversion is the need for solitude and alone time to recharge and rejuvenate. However, this need for solitude can sometimes be misunderstood by family members who may interpret it as a rejection or withdrawal. It is important for introverts to communicate their need for alone time to their family members and explain that it is not a reflection of their love or interest in them, but rather a necessary part of their self-care routine.

4.3.2 Balancing Quality Time and Alone Time

Finding a balance between spending quality time with family members and having enough alone time can be a delicate task for introverts. While introverts may enjoy spending time with their loved ones, they also need to ensure they have enough time to recharge. It is essential for introverts to communicate their needs to their family members and find a compromise that allows for both quality time together and sufficient alone time.

4.3.3 Understanding Different Communication Styles

Introverts and extroverts often have different communication styles, which can lead to misunderstandings within family dynamics. Introverts tend to be more reflective and thoughtful in their communication, while extroverts may be more spontaneous and talkative. It is important for family members to recognize and respect these differences in communication styles and find ways to bridge the gap. Introverts can benefit from expressing their thoughts and feelings in writing or through one-on-one conversations, where they feel more comfortable and heard.

4.3.4 Respecting Boundaries and Personal Space

Introverts highly value their personal space and boundaries. They may feel overwhelmed or drained when their personal space is invaded or when their boundaries are not respected. It is crucial for family members to understand and respect these boundaries, even if they may not fully comprehend the introvert's need for them. Open and honest communication about personal space and boundaries can help foster a more harmonious family environment.

4.3.5 Encouraging Individuality and Autonomy

Introverts often have a strong sense of individuality and autonomy. They may prefer to pursue their own interests and activities rather than constantly engaging in group or family activities. It is important for family members to support and encourage the introvert's individuality, allowing them the freedom to pursue their passions and interests. This can help introverts feel more accepted and understood within their family unit.

4.3.6 Building Emotional Connections

Introverts may struggle with building emotional connections within their family, especially if they feel misunderstood or overlooked. It is important for family members to create a safe and nurturing environment where introverts feel comfortable expressing their emotions and thoughts. Active listening, empathy, and validation are essential in building emotional connections with introverts. Family members can also engage in activities that introverts enjoy, such as reading, hiking, or having deep conversations, to foster a deeper emotional bond.

4.3.7 Encouraging Open Dialogue

Open and honest communication is vital in any family dynamic, but it is especially important for introverts who may struggle to express themselves verbally. Encouraging open dialogue within the family can help introverts feel more comfortable sharing their thoughts and feelings. Family members can create a safe space where everyone's opinions and perspectives are valued and respected, allowing introverts to contribute in their own unique way.

4.3.8 Seeking Professional Support

In some cases, family dynamics may become strained and challenging for introverts to navigate on their own. Seeking professional support, such as family therapy or counseling, can provide a safe and neutral space for family members to address their differences and work towards a more understanding and harmonious relationship. A trained therapist can help facilitate communication, provide tools for conflict resolution, and offer guidance on how to navigate the complexities of introvert-family dynamics.

In conclusion, introverts often face unique challenges within their family dynamics. It is crucial for both introverts and their family members to understand and respect each other's needs, boundaries, and communication styles. By fostering open dialogue, encouraging individuality, and seeking professional support when needed, introverts and their families can build stronger, more understanding relationships that celebrate and embrace the unique qualities of introversion.

4.4 Introverts and Work Relationships

Work relationships can be challenging for introverts, as they often find themselves in environments that prioritize extroverted qualities and behaviors. However, with a better understanding of their own needs and strengths, introverts can navigate these relationships and thrive in the workplace.

4.4.1 The Introvert's Communication Style

Introverts tend to have a different communication style compared to their extroverted counterparts. They often prefer to listen and observe before speaking, taking the time to process information internally. This can sometimes be misinterpreted as shyness or disinterest by others who are more accustomed to immediate and assertive communication.

In work relationships, it is important for introverts to find a balance between their natural inclination to listen and contribute their ideas. They can benefit from finding opportunities to express themselves in meetings or through written communication, where they can carefully articulate their thoughts and ideas.

4.4.2 Building Trust and Collaboration

Introverts value deep and meaningful connections, and this extends to their work relationships as well. They prefer to build trust and rapport with their colleagues before fully engaging in collaborative efforts. This can sometimes be misconstrued as aloofness or a lack of interest in teamwork.

To foster positive work relationships, introverts can take small steps to build trust with their colleagues. This can include actively listening, offering support, and showing genuine interest in their coworkers' ideas and perspectives. By demonstrating their commitment to the team and their willingness to contribute, introverts can establish themselves as valuable and reliable team members.

4.4.3 Managing Energy and Boundaries

One of the key challenges introverts face in work relationships is managing their energy levels. Extroverted work environments, with their constant social interactions and open office spaces, can be draining for introverts. It is crucial for introverts to prioritize self-care and set boundaries to protect their energy and well-being.

Introverts can create a conducive work environment by finding quiet spaces for focused work, taking regular breaks to recharge, and setting clear boundaries around their availability for social interactions. By communicating their needs respectfully and assertively, introverts can ensure that their colleagues understand and respect their boundaries.

4.4.4 Leveraging Introvert Strengths

While introverts may face challenges in work relationships, they also possess unique strengths that can contribute to their success in the workplace. Introverts are often excellent listeners and observers, which allows them to pick up on subtle cues and understand the dynamics within their teams. They are also known for their thoughtfulness, attention to detail, and ability to think deeply and critically.

Introverts can leverage these strengths by taking on roles that require careful analysis, problem-solving, and strategic thinking. They can excel in positions that allow them to work independently or in small groups, where they can fully utilize their creativity and focus. By recognizing and embracing their strengths, introverts can find fulfillment and success in their work relationships.

4.4.5 Nurturing Work-Life Balance

Maintaining a healthy work-life balance is essential for introverts to thrive in their work relationships. Introverts need time alone to recharge and reflect, and it is important for them to prioritize their well-being outside of work. This includes engaging in activities that bring them joy, practicing self-care, and setting aside time for solitude.

By nurturing their work-life balance, introverts can bring their best selves to their work relationships. They will have the energy and mental clarity to engage with their colleagues effectively and contribute meaningfully to their teams. Prioritizing self-care and setting boundaries between work and personal life allows introverts to maintain their well-being and avoid burnout.

In conclusion, introverts may face unique challenges in work relationships due to their different communication style and need for solitude. However, by understanding and embracing their introversion, introverts can navigate these relationships successfully. By leveraging their strengths, setting boundaries, and prioritizing self-care, introverts can thrive in the workplace and contribute their unique perspectives and talents.

5

Chapter 5

Embracing Introversion

5.1 Self-Acceptance as an Introvert

Self-acceptance is a crucial aspect of embracing introversion. As introverts, we often find ourselves misunderstood and labeled as "different" or "not like other people." These misconceptions can lead to feelings of inadequacy and a sense of not belonging. However, it is essential to recognize that being an introvert is not a flaw or something to be fixed; it is a unique and valuable trait.

5.1.1 Embracing Your Introverted Nature

To truly accept ourselves as introverts, we must first understand and appreciate the characteristics that make us who we are. Introversion is not a weakness; it is a natural temperament that brings with it a multitude of strengths and advantages. By acknowledging and embracing these qualities, we can begin to cultivate a sense of self-acceptance.

5.1.2 Recognizing the Power of Introversion

Introverts possess a deep capacity for introspection, creativity, and empathy. Our ability to reflect and think deeply allows us to approach problems from unique perspectives and find innovative solutions. By recognizing the power of introversion, we can harness these strengths and use them to our advantage in various aspects of our lives.

5.1.3 Overcoming Misunderstandings and Stereotypes

One of the biggest challenges introverts face is the misunderstanding and misinterpretation of our quiet and reserved nature. Society often values extroverted qualities such as assertiveness and sociability, leading to misconceptions about introverts being shy, antisocial, or lacking in social skills. It is crucial to challenge these stereotypes and educate others about the true nature of introversion.

5.1.4 Embracing Your Unique Perspective

As introverts, we have a unique way of experiencing the world. Our preference for solitude and introspection allows us to delve deep into our thoughts and emotions, gaining a profound understanding of ourselves and the world around us. Embracing this unique perspective can lead to personal growth and a greater appreciation for our introverted nature.

5.1.5 Cultivating Self-Compassion

Self-acceptance goes hand in hand with self-compassion. It is essential to be kind and understanding towards ourselves, recognizing that introversion is not a flaw but a beautiful aspect of our identity. Practicing self-compassion involves treating ourselves with love, patience, and understanding, especially during times when we may feel overwhelmed or misunderstood.

5.1.6 Building a Supportive Network

Surrounding ourselves with understanding and supportive individuals is crucial for self-acceptance as introverts. Building a network of like-minded individuals who appreciate and value our introverted nature can provide a sense of belonging and validation. These individuals can offer support, understanding, and encouragement, helping us navigate the challenges that come with being introverted in an extroverted world.

5.1.7 Celebrating Your Introversion

Instead of viewing introversion as a limitation, we should celebrate and embrace it as a unique and valuable trait. By recognizing and appreciating the strengths and advantages that come with introversion, we can cultivate a sense of pride in our identity. Celebrating our introversion allows us to fully accept ourselves and live authentically, without feeling the need to conform to societal expectations.

5.1.8 Practicing Self-Care and Setting Boundaries

Self-acceptance also involves prioritizing self-care and setting boundaries. As introverts, we need time alone to recharge and rejuvenate. It is essential to listen to our needs and give ourselves permission to take breaks when necessary. Setting boundaries with others and communicating our needs effectively can help us maintain a healthy balance between social interactions and solitude.

5.1.9 Embracing Growth and Personal Development

Self-acceptance does not mean stagnation; it is a continuous journey of growth and personal development. By embracing our introversion, we can explore ways to enhance our strengths, develop new skills, and expand our comfort zones. This process allows us to grow as individuals while staying true to our introverted nature.

5.1.10 Finding Fulfillment as an Introvert

Ultimately, self-acceptance as an introvert leads to a sense of fulfillment and contentment. By embracing our introverted nature, recognizing our strengths, and surrounding ourselves with understanding individuals, we can create a life that aligns with our values and brings us joy. Finding fulfillment as an introvert involves embracing our unique qualities and living authentically, without feeling the need to conform to societal expectations.

In conclusion, self-acceptance as an introvert is a transformative journey that involves embracing our unique qualities, challenging misconceptions, and cultivating a sense of pride in our identity. By recognizing the power of introversion, practicing self-compassion, and surrounding ourselves with supportive individuals, we can navigate the challenges of an extroverted world while staying true to ourselves. Embracing our introverted nature allows us to find fulfillment, live authentically, and celebrate the strengths that make us who we are.

5.2 Setting Boundaries and Prioritizing Self-Care

Introverts often find themselves in situations where they feel overwhelmed or drained by social interactions. This can be due to the fact that introverts gain energy from solitude and introspection, rather than from external stimuli. As a result, it is crucial for introverts to set boundaries and prioritize self-care in order to maintain their well-being and thrive in an extroverted world.

5.2.1 Understanding the Importance of Setting Boundaries

Setting boundaries is essential for introverts to protect their energy and maintain a healthy balance in their lives. It involves clearly communicating their needs and limitations to others, and establishing limits on the amount of social interaction they can handle. By setting boundaries, introverts can create a safe space for themselves where they can recharge and rejuvenate.

One aspect of setting boundaries is learning to say "no" when necessary. Introverts often feel pressured to participate in social activities or events that they may not be comfortable with. However, it is important for introverts to recognize their own limits and prioritize their well-being. Saying "no" allows introverts to conserve their energy and focus on activities that align with their interests and values.

5.2.2 Establishing Self-Care Practices

Prioritizing self-care is crucial for introverts to maintain their mental, emotional, and physical well-being. Self-care involves engaging in activities that promote relaxation, rejuvenation, and personal growth. It is a way for introverts to recharge their energy and nurture their inner selves.

One important aspect of self-care for introverts is creating a daily routine that includes time for solitude and reflection. This can involve setting aside specific periods of the day where introverts can engage in activities that bring them joy and peace, such as reading, writing, or practicing mindfulness. By incorporating these moments of solitude into their daily lives, introverts can replenish their energy and find inner balance.

Additionally, introverts can benefit from engaging in activities that align with their interests and passions. This can include hobbies, creative pursuits, or engaging in solitary activities that bring them joy. By dedicating time to these activities, introverts can tap into their creativity and find fulfillment in their own unique way.

5.2.3 Communicating Boundaries and Self-Care Needs

Effectively communicating boundaries and self-care needs is essential for introverts to navigate their relationships and social interactions. It is important for introverts to express their needs and limitations to their friends, family, and colleagues in a clear and assertive manner.

When communicating boundaries, introverts can use "I" statements to express their feelings and needs. For example, instead of saying, "You always invite me to social events, and I don't want to go," introverts can say, "I appreciate your invitations, but I need some alone time to recharge. I hope you understand." By using "I" statements, introverts can express their boundaries without placing blame on others.

It is also important for introverts to educate those around them about introversion and its unique characteristics. By explaining their need for solitude and introspection, introverts can help others understand their perspective and foster more supportive and understanding relationships.

5.2.4 Seeking Support and Building a Supportive Network

Building a supportive network is crucial for introverts to thrive in an extroverted world. This network can consist of like-minded individuals who understand and respect introversion, as well as individuals who appreciate the unique strengths introverts bring to the table.

Introverts can seek support from friends, family, or support groups that cater to introverts. These individuals can provide a safe space for introverts to share their experiences, seek advice, and receive validation. Additionally, joining online communities or forums dedicated to introversion can also provide a sense of belonging and support.

In conclusion, setting boundaries and prioritizing self-care are essential for introverts to navigate their lives and thrive in an extroverted world. By clearly communicating their needs, establishing self-care practices, and seeking support, introverts can create a balanced and fulfilling life that embraces their unique qualities. It is through these actions that introverts can truly embrace their introversion and find happiness and success on their own terms.

5.3 Finding Balance in an Extroverted World

Introverts often find themselves navigating a world that seems to be designed for extroverts. From social gatherings to workplace dynamics, the extroverted world can sometimes feel overwhelming and draining for introverts. However, finding balance is essential for introverts to thrive and make the most of their unique strengths. In this section, we will explore strategies and techniques that can help introverts find balance in an extroverted world.

5.3.1 Understanding the Extroverted World

To find balance, it is crucial for introverts to understand the extroverted world they live in. Extroversion is often celebrated and valued in society, with extroverted traits such as assertiveness, sociability, and outgoingness being highly praised. This can create a sense of pressure for introverts to conform to extroverted norms and behaviors.

However, it is important to recognize that introversion is not a flaw or a weakness. Introverts have their own unique strengths, such as deep thinking, creativity, and empathy. By understanding and embracing these strengths, introverts can navigate the extroverted world with confidence and authenticity.

5.3.2 Setting Personal Boundaries

One of the key strategies for finding balance as an introvert is setting personal boundaries. Introverts often need time alone to recharge and reflect, and it is essential to prioritize this need. This may involve saying no to social events or activities that feel overwhelming or draining.

Setting boundaries can also extend to managing energy levels throughout the day. Introverts may find it helpful to schedule breaks or quiet time during the day to recharge and prevent overstimulation. By setting clear boundaries and honoring their own needs, introverts can maintain a healthy balance between social interactions and solitude.

5.3.3 Finding Introvert-Friendly Activities

In an extroverted world, it can be challenging for introverts to find activities that align with their preferences and needs. However, there are plenty of introvert-friendly activities that can provide a sense of fulfillment and rejuvenation.

Introverts often thrive in activities that allow for introspection and creativity. Reading, writing, painting, gardening, or engaging in hobbies that involve solitary pursuits can be incredibly rewarding for introverts. These activities provide an opportunity for self-expression and allow introverts to recharge in their own unique way.

5.3.4 Cultivating Meaningful Connections

While introverts may prefer deep and meaningful connections over large social circles, it is still important for them to cultivate relationships that bring joy and fulfillment. Building a support network of like-minded individuals who understand and appreciate introversion can be invaluable.

Introverts can seek out communities, groups, or organizations that align with their interests and values. These spaces provide an opportunity to connect with others who share similar perspectives and experiences. By surrounding themselves with understanding and supportive individuals, introverts can find a sense of belonging and acceptance in an extroverted world.

5.3.5 Practicing Self-Care

Self-care is essential for introverts to maintain balance and well-being. Taking care of one's physical, mental, and emotional health is crucial in navigating an extroverted world. This may involve practicing mindfulness, engaging in relaxation techniques, or pursuing activities that bring joy and rejuvenation.

Introverts can also benefit from creating a daily self-care routine that includes activities such as meditation, journaling, or engaging in hobbies. By prioritizing self-care, introverts can recharge their energy and maintain a healthy balance between social interactions and solitude.

5.3.6 Seeking Support and Understanding

Finding balance in an extroverted world can be challenging, and introverts may sometimes feel misunderstood or isolated. Seeking support from understanding friends, family, or even professional counselors can provide a safe space to express feelings and concerns.

Additionally, joining online communities or support groups specifically for introverts can be a valuable resource. These platforms offer a sense of belonging and understanding, allowing introverts to connect with others who share similar experiences and challenges.

5.3.7 Embracing Flexibility and Adaptability

While finding balance is important, it is also essential for introverts to embrace flexibility and adaptability. The extroverted world is constantly changing, and introverts may need to navigate various social situations and environments.

By embracing flexibility, introverts can learn to adapt their communication styles and social behaviors when necessary. This does not mean compromising their introverted nature but rather finding ways to navigate the extroverted world while staying true to themselves.

5.3.8 Celebrating Introversion

Lastly, it is crucial for introverts to celebrate their introversion and recognize the unique strengths they bring to the world. Introverts have a valuable perspective and contribute in meaningful ways, even in an extroverted society.

By embracing their introversion and advocating for its importance, introverts can help shift societal perceptions and create a more inclusive and understanding world. Celebrating introversion not only benefits introverts themselves but also promotes a more diverse and balanced society.

In conclusion, finding balance in an extroverted world is a journey that introverts embark on. By understanding the extroverted world, setting personal boundaries, engaging in introvert-friendly activities, cultivating meaningful connections, practicing self-care, seeking support, embracing flexibility, and celebrating introversion, introverts can navigate the extroverted world with confidence, authenticity, and a sense of fulfillment.

5.4 Harnessing the Strengths of Introversion

Introversion is often misunderstood and undervalued in a society that tends to prioritize extroverted qualities. However, introverts possess a unique set of strengths that can be harnessed and utilized to their advantage. In this section, we will explore some of these strengths and how introverts can leverage them to thrive in various aspects of life.

5.4.1 Deep Thinking and Reflection

One of the greatest strengths of introverts is their ability to engage in deep thinking and reflection. Introverts tend to have rich inner worlds and spend a significant amount of time processing their thoughts and ideas. This introspective nature allows introverts to delve into complex problems, analyze situations from multiple perspectives, and come up with innovative solutions. By harnessing this strength, introverts can excel in fields that require critical thinking, such as research, writing, and problem-solving.

5.4.2 Active Listening and Empathy

Introverts are known for their exceptional listening skills and ability to empathize with others. They have a natural inclination to listen attentively and understand the emotions and needs of those around them. This strength enables introverts to build deep and meaningful connections with others, as they genuinely care about the well-being of those they interact with. By harnessing their active listening and empathy, introverts can excel in professions that involve counseling, coaching, and mentoring.

5.4.3 Creativity and Imagination

Introverts often possess a rich inner world filled with creativity and imagination. They have a unique ability to tap into their imagination and come up with original ideas and concepts. This strength allows introverts to excel in artistic pursuits, such as writing, painting, music, and other creative endeavors. By embracing their creativity and imagination, introverts can bring a fresh perspective to the world and make significant contributions in the fields of art, design, and innovation.

5.4.4 Focus and Attention to Detail

Introverts are known for their ability to concentrate deeply and pay attention to detail. They thrive in environments that allow them to work independently and dive into tasks that require precision and meticulousness. This strength enables introverts to excel in professions that demand focus and attention to detail, such as research, programming, accounting, and data analysis. By harnessing their focus and attention to detail, introverts can achieve remarkable results and make valuable contributions in their chosen fields.

5.4.5 Problem-Solving and Decision-Making

Introverts possess excellent problem-solving and decision-making skills. They approach challenges with a thoughtful and analytical mindset, carefully considering all the available information before arriving at a conclusion. Introverts are often skilled at weighing the pros and cons, identifying potential risks, and making well-informed decisions. This strength allows introverts to excel in leadership roles, where their thoughtful and strategic approach can lead to effective problem-solving and decision-making.

5.4.6 Independence and Self-Reliance

Introverts thrive in solitude and are comfortable with their own company. They have a strong sense of independence and self-reliance, which allows them to work autonomously and take ownership of their tasks and responsibilities. This strength enables introverts to excel in entrepreneurial ventures, freelancing, and other independent work settings. By harnessing their independence and self-reliance, introverts can create their own paths and find fulfillment in pursuing their passions.

5.4.7 Ability to Connect on a Deeper Level

Introverts have a unique ability to connect with others on a deeper level. They value meaningful conversations and prefer quality over quantity when it comes to relationships. Introverts are often sought after for their wisdom, insight, and ability to provide genuine support and understanding. By harnessing their ability to connect on a deeper level, introverts can cultivate strong and lasting relationships that bring joy and fulfillment to their lives.

In conclusion, introverts possess a wide range of strengths that can be harnessed and utilized to their advantage. By embracing their deep thinking, active listening, creativity, focus, problem-solving skills, independence, and ability to connect on a deeper level, introverts can thrive in various aspects of life. It is essential for introverts to recognize and celebrate their unique strengths, as they have the power to make a significant impact in the world.

6

Chapter 6

Overcoming Challenges

6.1 Dealing with Misunderstandings and Stereotypes

Introverts often find themselves facing misunderstandings and stereotypes due to their unique nature and preference for solitude. These misconceptions can come from friends, family, colleagues, or even romantic partners who may not fully understand or appreciate the introvert's needs and characteristics. In this section, we will explore some common misunderstandings and stereotypes that introverts encounter and discuss strategies for dealing with them.

6.1.1 The "You're Not Like Other People" Stereotype

One common stereotype that introverts often encounter is the belief that they are somehow different or abnormal compared to extroverts. This stereotype can manifest in comments like, "You're not like other people" or "Why don't you enjoy socializing like everyone else?" While these comments may be well-intentioned, they can be hurtful and reinforce the idea that introverts are somehow flawed or need to change.

It is important for introverts to remember that their introversion is not a defect or something to be fixed. Introversion is a natural personality trait that is present in approximately one-third to one-half of the population. It is a valid and valuable way of being in the world, and introverts should embrace and celebrate their unique qualities.

6.1.2 Responding to Misunderstandings

When faced with misunderstandings or stereotypes, it can be challenging for introverts to respond effectively. Here are some strategies that can help:

1. **Educate and Explain**: Take the opportunity to educate others about introversion and explain what it means to be an introvert. Share information about the introvert's need for solitude, preference for deep conversations, and ability to thrive in quieter environments. By providing this knowledge, you can help others understand and appreciate your perspective.
2. **Communicate Your Needs**: Clearly communicate your needs to those around you. Let them know that you require alone time to recharge and that socializing in large groups can be draining for you. By expressing your needs, you can help others understand why you may decline certain invitations or prefer quieter activities.
3. **Set Boundaries**: Establishing boundaries is crucial for

introverts. Let others know when you need space and time alone, and be assertive in protecting your boundaries. This can help prevent misunderstandings and ensure that your needs are respected.

4. **Share Personal Experiences**: Share your personal experiences as an introvert to help others relate and understand your perspective better. By sharing stories of how you thrive in quieter environments or how you find solace in introspection, you can help break down stereotypes and foster empathy.

5. **Seek Support**: Surround yourself with supportive individuals who understand and appreciate your introverted nature. Seek out like-minded individuals who can provide validation and support during times of misunderstanding or frustration.

6.1.3 Challenging Stereotypes

Challenging stereotypes is an ongoing process that requires patience and persistence. Here are some ways to challenge stereotypes as an introvert:

1. **Lead by Example**: Show others that introverts can be successful, happy, and fulfilled individuals. By living your life authentically and embracing your introversion, you can inspire others to question their preconceived notions about introverts.

2. **Share Success Stories**: Share success stories of introverts who have achieved great things in various fields. Highlight the accomplishments of introverted leaders, artists, scientists, and innovators to demonstrate that introversion is

not a barrier to success.

3. **Advocate for Introversion**: Take an active role in advocating for introversion. Speak up in discussions about personality types and challenge misconceptions whenever you can. By sharing your knowledge and experiences, you can help dispel stereotypes and promote a more inclusive understanding of introversion.

4. **Promote Self-Acceptance**: Encourage self-acceptance among fellow introverts. Help others embrace their introverted nature and recognize the strengths and unique qualities that come with it. By promoting self-acceptance, you can create a supportive community that challenges stereotypes and fosters personal growth.

Remember, overcoming misunderstandings and stereotypes takes time and effort. By educating others, communicating your needs, and challenging stereotypes, you can help create a more understanding and accepting world for introverts. Embrace your introversion, celebrate your uniqueness, and remember that you are not alone in your journey.

6.2 Managing Overstimulation and Burnout

Introverts often find themselves facing the challenge of managing overstimulation and burnout in a world that seems designed for extroverts. The constant noise, social interactions, and external stimuli can be overwhelming for introverts, leading to exhaustion and a need for solitude. In this section, we will explore strategies and techniques that introverts can use to effectively manage overstimulation and prevent burnout.

6.2.1 Understanding Overstimulation

Overstimulation occurs when an introvert's sensory input exceeds their capacity to process it. This can happen in various situations, such as crowded environments, loud noises, or prolonged social interactions. Unlike extroverts who thrive in stimulating environments, introverts may feel drained and overwhelmed in these situations.

It is important for introverts to recognize the signs of overstimulation, which may include fatigue, irritability, difficulty concentrating, and a strong desire to withdraw from social interactions. By understanding these signs, introverts can take proactive steps to manage their energy levels and prevent burnout.

6.2.2 Creating a Calming Environment

One effective way for introverts to manage overstimulation is by creating a calming environment. This can be a designated space in their home or workplace where they can retreat to when feeling overwhelmed. The environment should be quiet, clutter-free, and filled with objects that bring a sense of peace and tranquility, such as soft lighting, comfortable seating, and calming scents.

Additionally, introverts can incorporate activities into their daily routine that promote relaxation and reduce stress. This can include practicing mindfulness or meditation, engaging in hobbies that provide a sense of calm, or simply taking quiet walks in nature. By intentionally creating a calming environment and engaging in activities that promote relaxation, introverts can recharge and prevent burnout.

6.2.3 Setting Boundaries

Setting boundaries is crucial for introverts to manage over-stimulation and prevent burnout. Introverts often feel pressured to participate in social activities or engage in prolonged interactions, even when they are feeling overwhelmed. It is important for introverts to assertively communicate their needs and limitations to others, explaining that they require time alone to recharge.

By setting boundaries, introverts can create a balance between social interactions and solitude, ensuring that they have enough time to recharge their energy. This may involve politely declining invitations to social events, scheduling regular alone time in their calendar, or communicating their need for breaks during group activities. Setting boundaries allows introverts to prioritize their well-being and prevent overstimulation.

6.2.4 Practicing Self-Care

Self-care is essential for introverts to manage overstimulation and prevent burnout. This involves taking care of one's physical, emotional, and mental well-being. Introverts can prioritize self-care by engaging in activities that recharge their energy and bring them joy.

For introverts, self-care may include activities such as reading a book, taking a long bath, practicing yoga or meditation, journaling, or engaging in creative pursuits. It is important for introverts to listen to their own needs and give themselves permission to prioritize self-care without feeling guilty or selfish.

6.2.5 Time Management and Prioritization

Effective time management and prioritization are key for introverts to prevent overstimulation and burnout. Introverts often have limited energy reserves, and it is important for them to allocate their time and energy wisely.

Introverts can benefit from creating a schedule that allows for regular breaks and alone time. This may involve blocking off specific periods in their day for solitude and reflection. By prioritizing activities that align with their values and recharge their energy, introverts can prevent overstimulation and ensure that they have enough energy for the things that matter most to them.

6.2.6 Seeking Support and Understanding

Lastly, introverts can benefit from seeking support and understanding from others. It can be helpful to surround oneself with individuals who appreciate and respect introversion. This can include friends, family members, or support groups who understand the need for solitude and can provide a safe space for introverts to recharge.

Additionally, seeking professional help, such as therapy or counseling, can be beneficial for introverts who are struggling with overstimulation and burnout. A therapist can provide guidance and strategies tailored to the individual's needs, helping them navigate the challenges of managing overstimulation in an extroverted world.

By implementing these strategies and techniques, introverts can effectively manage overstimulation, prevent burnout, and thrive in a world that may not always understand their unique needs and preferences. It is important for introverts to prioritize self-care, set boundaries, and create a supportive environment that allows them to embrace their introversion and live authentically.

6.3 Building Confidence as an Introvert

Building confidence as an introvert can be a challenging journey, especially in a world that often values extroverted qualities. However, it is important to remember that introversion is not a flaw or a weakness. It is a unique personality trait that comes with its own set of strengths and advantages. By understanding and embracing our introversion, we can build confidence and thrive in both personal and professional settings.

6.3.1 Embracing Self-Acceptance

The first step in building confidence as an introvert is to embrace self-acceptance. It is crucial to recognize that introversion is a natural and valid way of being. Instead of trying to change ourselves to fit societal expectations, we should focus on accepting and appreciating our introverted nature.

Self-acceptance involves acknowledging our introverted tendencies, such as needing alone time to recharge, preferring deep conversations over small talk, and enjoying solitary activities. By accepting these traits as part of who we are, we can begin to build confidence in our own unique strengths and abilities.

6.3.2 Stepping Out of the Comfort Zone

While introverts may feel more comfortable in solitude or with a small group of close friends, it is important to challenge ourselves and step out of our comfort zones from time to time. Building confidence often requires pushing past our perceived limitations and trying new experiences.

This does not mean that introverts need to become extroverts or completely change their personalities. Instead, it means gradually exposing ourselves to new social situations and gradually expanding our comfort zones. This could involve attending social events, joining clubs or organizations that align with our interests, or taking on leadership roles that allow us to showcase our unique strengths.

6.3.3 Cultivating Positive Self-Talk

Confidence begins with the way we talk to ourselves. As introverts, we may be prone to self-doubt and negative self-talk. To build confidence, it is important to cultivate positive self-talk and challenge our inner critic.

Instead of focusing on our perceived weaknesses or comparing ourselves to extroverted individuals, we should celebrate our introverted strengths. Remind yourself of the times when your introversion has served you well, such as your ability to listen attentively, think deeply, and bring a unique perspective to discussions. By reframing our thoughts and focusing on our positive qualities, we can boost our confidence and self-esteem.

6.3.4 Seeking Support and Connection

Building confidence as an introvert does not mean going through the journey alone. Seeking support and connection from like-minded individuals can be incredibly empowering. Surrounding ourselves with people who understand and appreciate our introverted nature can provide a sense of validation and encouragement.

This support can come from joining introvert communities, attending meetups or workshops specifically designed for introverts, or seeking out mentors who have successfully navigated the challenges of introversion. By connecting with others who share similar experiences, we can gain valuable insights, learn from their journeys, and build confidence together.

6.3.5 Practicing Self-Care

Self-care plays a crucial role in building confidence as an introvert. Taking care of our physical, mental, and emotional well-being is essential for maintaining a positive mindset and a strong sense of self.

For introverts, self-care often involves creating space for solitude and reflection. This could mean setting aside regular alone time to recharge, engaging in activities that bring us joy and relaxation, and prioritizing our own needs and boundaries. By practicing self-care, we can replenish our energy, reduce stress, and cultivate a sense of inner peace, which in turn boosts our confidence.

6.3.6 Celebrating Personal Achievements

Finally, building confidence as an introvert involves celebrating our personal achievements, no matter how small they may seem. It is important to acknowledge and appreciate our progress along the way.

Whether it's successfully navigating a social event, speaking up in a meeting, or taking on a new challenge, each step forward is a testament to our growth and resilience. By recognizing and celebrating our accomplishments, we reinforce our belief in our abilities and build a strong foundation of confidence.

Remember, building confidence as an introvert is a journey that takes time and patience. It is about embracing our introverted nature, stepping out of our comfort zones, cultivating positive self-talk, seeking support, practicing self-care, and celebrating our achievements. By doing so, we can build a deep sense of confidence that allows us to thrive as unique and valuable individuals in an extroverted world.

6.4 Navigating Career Challenges as an Introvert

Introverts often face unique challenges in the workplace due to their preference for solitude and introspection. While extroverts thrive in social and fast-paced environments, introverts may find it more difficult to navigate the demands of a career that values constant interaction and assertiveness. However, with a better understanding of their own strengths and strategies for success, introverts can overcome these challenges and excel in their chosen fields.

6.4.1 Finding the Right Work Environment

One of the first steps in navigating career challenges as an introvert is finding the right work environment. Introverts tend to thrive in quieter and more focused settings, where they can work independently and have the time and space for deep thinking. It is important for introverts to consider the culture and atmosphere of a potential workplace before accepting a job offer. Look for companies that value individual contributions, provide opportunities for solitude, and promote a healthy work-life balance.

6.4.2 Leveraging Introvert Strengths

Introverts possess a unique set of strengths that can be leveraged to excel in their careers. These strengths include excellent listening skills, attention to detail, and the ability to think deeply and critically. Introverts often excel in roles that require analysis, research, and problem-solving. By recognizing and embracing these strengths, introverts can position themselves for success in their chosen fields.

6.4.3 Networking for Introverts

Networking can be a daunting task for introverts, as it often involves large social gatherings and small talk. However, networking is an essential part of career growth and can lead to valuable opportunities. Introverts can navigate networking challenges by focusing on quality over quantity. Instead of attending every event, introverts can choose a few select gatherings where they feel comfortable and can engage in meaningful conversations. Additionally, introverts can leverage their listening skills to ask thoughtful questions and show genuine interest in others, which can leave a lasting impression.

6.4.4 Effective Communication Strategies

Communication is a vital skill in any career, and introverts may need to develop strategies to effectively communicate their ideas and contributions. Introverts often excel in written communication, so utilizing email or other written forms of communication can be a valuable tool. Additionally, introverts can prepare in advance for meetings or presentations, allowing them to gather their thoughts and present their ideas in a clear and concise manner. It is also important for introverts to find their voice and advocate for themselves when necessary, even if it may feel uncomfortable at times.

6.4.5 Managing Energy and Avoiding Burnout

Introverts can easily become overwhelmed by the demands of a busy and extroverted workplace. It is crucial for introverts to prioritize self-care and manage their energy levels to avoid burnout. This can be achieved by taking regular breaks, finding moments of solitude throughout the day, and engaging in activities that recharge their energy, such as reading or taking walks. Setting boundaries and learning to say no when necessary is also essential for introverts to maintain a healthy work–life balance.

6.4.6 Seeking Introvert-Friendly Roles

While introverts can excel in a variety of careers, certain roles may be more naturally suited to their strengths and preferences. Introverts may find fulfillment in careers that allow for deep focus and independent work, such as writing, research, programming, or graphic design. By seeking out roles that align with their natural inclinations, introverts can find greater satisfaction and success in their careers.

6.4.7 Embracing Continuous Learning and Growth

As with any career, introverts should embrace continuous learning and growth to stay relevant and advance in their chosen fields. This can involve attending workshops or conferences, pursuing additional education or certifications, or seeking out mentors who can provide guidance and support. By investing in their professional development, introverts can enhance their skills and increase their confidence, ultimately opening doors to new opportunities.

6.4.8 Building a Supportive Network

Building a supportive network is crucial for introverts to navigate career challenges. This network can consist of like-minded individuals who understand and appreciate introversion, as well as mentors and colleagues who can provide guidance and support. Engaging in professional associations or online communities can be a valuable way for introverts to connect with others who share similar experiences and challenges.

In conclusion, while introverts may face unique challenges

in their careers, they can navigate these challenges by finding the right work environment, leveraging their strengths, developing effective communication strategies, managing their energy, seeking introvert-friendly roles, embracing continuous learning, and building a supportive network. By understanding and embracing their introversion, introverts can thrive in their careers and find fulfillment and success on their own terms.

7

Chapter 7

Thriving as an Introvert

7.1 Creating an Introvert-Friendly Environment

Creating an environment that is conducive to introverts is essential for their well-being and overall happiness. Introverts thrive in spaces that allow them to recharge, reflect, and engage in activities that align with their unique needs and preferences. In this section, we will explore various strategies and tips for creating an introvert-friendly environment that fosters their growth and supports their individuality.

7.1.1 Designing a Calm and Quiet Space

One of the key aspects of an introvert-friendly environment is the presence of a calm and quiet space. Introverts often find solace in peaceful surroundings where they can retreat and recharge their energy. Designating a specific area in your home or workplace that is free from distractions and noise can greatly benefit introverts. This space can be a cozy corner with comfortable seating, soft lighting, and minimal visual stimulation. By creating a peaceful environment, introverts can find the solitude they need to reflect, think, and recharge.

7.1.2 Allowing for Personal Space and Boundaries

Respecting personal space and boundaries is crucial when creating an introvert-friendly environment. Introverts value their alone time and may feel overwhelmed when their personal space is invaded or when they are constantly surrounded by people. It is important to establish clear boundaries and communicate them effectively to those around you. This can include setting aside specific times for solitude, establishing quiet hours, or simply asking for privacy when needed. By respecting these boundaries, introverts can feel more comfortable and at ease in their environment.

7.1.3 Providing Opportunities for Reflection and Introspection

Introverts thrive on introspection and deep thinking. Creating an environment that encourages and supports these activities can greatly benefit introverts. Consider incorporating elements such as comfortable seating, natural lighting, and calming decor that promotes relaxation and reflection. Providing resources such as books, journals, or art supplies can also encourage introverts to engage in activities that stimulate their creativity and allow for self-expression. By providing opportunities for reflection and introspection, introverts can tap into their inner world and gain a deeper understanding of themselves.

7.1.4 Offering Flexible Work and Study Options

Many introverts find it challenging to thrive in traditional work or study environments that are heavily focused on group activities and constant social interaction. Creating an introvert-friendly environment in these settings involves offering flexible options that cater to their needs. This can include providing quiet spaces for focused work or study, allowing for flexible schedules that accommodate introverts' preferred working hours, and promoting a culture that values individual contributions and independent thinking. By offering these options, introverts can feel more comfortable and productive in their work or study environment.

7.1.5 Encouraging Meaningful and Deep Conversations

Introverts often prefer quality over quantity when it comes to social interactions. They thrive on meaningful and deep conversations rather than small talk. Creating an introvert-friendly environment involves fostering an atmosphere that encourages these types of conversations. This can be achieved by organizing discussion groups or book clubs centered around topics of interest, providing opportunities for one-on-one conversations, or creating online platforms where introverts can connect and engage in meaningful discussions. By encouraging these types of interactions, introverts can feel more connected and understood in their environment.

7.1.6 Promoting Flexibility and Autonomy

Introverts value autonomy and the ability to work or engage in activities at their own pace. Creating an introvert-friendly environment involves promoting flexibility and allowing introverts to have control over their time and tasks. This can be achieved by offering flexible work hours, allowing for remote work options, or providing opportunities for introverts to work independently on projects that align with their strengths and interests. By promoting flexibility and autonomy, introverts can feel empowered and motivated to excel in their environment.

7.1.7 Minimizing Overstimulation and Noise

Introverts are highly sensitive to external stimuli and can easily become overwhelmed in noisy or overstimulating environments. Creating an introvert-friendly environment involves minimizing unnecessary noise and distractions. This can be achieved by implementing soundproofing measures, using noise-cancelling headphones, or creating designated quiet areas where introverts can retreat when they need a break from sensory overload. By minimizing overstimulation and noise, introverts can feel more comfortable and focused in their environment.

7.1.8 Embracing Technology for Communication

Introverts often find it easier to express themselves through written communication rather than face-to-face interactions. Creating an introvert-friendly environment involves embracing technology as a means of communication. This can include utilizing email, instant messaging, or video conferencing platforms that allow introverts to communicate in a way that feels more comfortable for them. By embracing technology, introverts can feel more confident and at ease when expressing their thoughts and ideas.

Creating an introvert-friendly environment is not only beneficial for introverts themselves but also for the overall productivity and well-being of everyone involved. By understanding and accommodating the unique needs of introverts, we can create spaces that foster their growth, creativity, and happiness.

7.2 Finding Meaningful Connections

Introverts often face challenges when it comes to finding meaningful connections with others. Their preference for solitude and deep introspection can sometimes be misunderstood by those who are more extroverted. However, it is important for introverts to remember that they are not alone in their quest for meaningful connections. There are ways for introverts to navigate social interactions and build relationships that align with their unique needs and preferences.

7.2.1 The Importance of Authenticity

One of the keys to finding meaningful connections as an introvert is embracing authenticity. Introverts thrive when they can be their true selves and engage in genuine conversations. It is important to remember that it is okay to be introverted and to embrace the qualities that make you unique. By being authentic, introverts can attract like-minded individuals who appreciate and understand their need for solitude and deep connections.

7.2.2 Seeking Out Like-Minded Individuals

Finding meaningful connections often involves seeking out like-minded individuals who share similar interests and values. Introverts can benefit from joining groups or communities that align with their passions and hobbies. This allows them to connect with others who understand and appreciate their introverted nature. Whether it's joining a book club, attending a yoga class, or participating in online forums, introverts can find solace in connecting with others who share their interests.

7.2.3 Quality over Quantity

Introverts often prefer deep and meaningful connections over superficial interactions. They value quality over quantity when it comes to relationships. Instead of trying to maintain a large circle of friends, introverts may find more fulfillment in cultivating a few close and meaningful friendships. These deep connections provide introverts with the emotional support and understanding they crave.

7.2.4 Building Connections through Shared Activities

Introverts may find it easier to connect with others through shared activities rather than traditional social settings. Engaging in activities that align with their interests allows introverts to bond with others in a more natural and comfortable way. Whether it's hiking, painting, or attending a cooking class, participating in activities that bring joy and fulfillment can lead to meaningful connections with others who share similar passions.

7.2.5 Embracing Online Communities

The rise of technology and social media has provided introverts with new opportunities to connect with others. Online communities and forums allow introverts to engage in conversations and build relationships from the comfort of their own homes. These virtual spaces provide a platform for introverts to express themselves and connect with like-minded individuals who understand and appreciate their introverted nature.

7.2.6 Cultivating Deep Listening Skills

Introverts excel in the art of deep listening. By honing their listening skills, introverts can create meaningful connections with others. Taking the time to truly listen and understand others' perspectives fosters a sense of trust and mutual respect. This allows introverts to build strong and meaningful connections with others, as they are able to provide a safe space for individuals to share their thoughts and feelings.

7.2.7 Practicing Vulnerability

Building meaningful connections often requires vulnerability. Introverts may find it challenging to open up and share their innermost thoughts and feelings. However, by practicing vulnerability, introverts can create deeper connections with others. Sharing personal experiences and emotions allows others to see the authentic and genuine side of introverts, fostering a sense of trust and intimacy in relationships.

7.2.8 Nurturing Existing Relationships

While introverts may prefer solitude, it is important for them to nurture and maintain their existing relationships. Taking the time to check in with loved ones and show appreciation for their presence in their lives can strengthen the bond between introverts and their loved ones. By investing in their relationships, introverts can create a support system that understands and respects their introverted nature.

7.2.9 Seeking Professional Help

In some cases, introverts may struggle to find meaningful connections due to underlying social anxiety or other mental health challenges. Seeking professional help, such as therapy or counseling, can provide introverts with the tools and support they need to navigate social interactions and build meaningful connections. A therapist can help introverts explore their fears and insecurities, develop coping strategies, and build self-confidence in social settings.

7.2.10 Embracing Self-Acceptance

Ultimately, finding meaningful connections as an introvert starts with self-acceptance. Embracing and celebrating one's introverted nature allows introverts to attract individuals who appreciate and understand them. By valuing their unique qualities and prioritizing their own needs, introverts can build relationships that bring joy, fulfillment, and understanding into their lives.

Finding meaningful connections as an introvert may require

some effort and self-reflection, but it is a journey worth embarking on. By embracing authenticity, seeking out like-minded individuals, and nurturing existing relationships, introverts can create a fulfilling social network that aligns with their introverted nature. Remember, being an introvert is not a limitation, but rather a unique and valuable trait that can lead to deep and meaningful connections with others.

7.3 Developing a Personal Growth Plan

As an introvert, it is essential to recognize and embrace your unique qualities and strengths. Developing a personal growth plan can help you navigate the challenges and maximize the opportunities that come with being an introvert. This plan will serve as a roadmap for your personal and professional development, allowing you to thrive in an extroverted world while staying true to yourself.

7.3.1 Reflecting on Your Values and Goals

To begin developing your personal growth plan, take some time to reflect on your values and goals. What is truly important to you? What do you want to achieve in your life? Understanding your values and goals will provide a solid foundation for your personal growth journey.

Consider the areas of your life that you would like to focus on, such as career, relationships, personal well-being, or hobbies. Think about what success means to you in each of these areas and how you can align your actions with your values and goals.

7.3.2 Identifying Strengths and Areas for Improvement

Next, it is important to assess your strengths and areas for improvement. As an introvert, you possess unique qualities that can be leveraged to your advantage. These may include deep thinking, empathy, creativity, and the ability to listen attentively. Recognizing and embracing these strengths will boost your confidence and help you excel in various aspects of your life.

At the same time, identify areas where you feel you could improve. This could be anything from public speaking skills to assertiveness or networking abilities. Remember that personal growth is a continuous process, and there is always room for improvement. By acknowledging these areas, you can create a plan to develop and enhance these skills.

7.3.3 Setting SMART Goals

Once you have reflected on your values, goals, strengths, and areas for improvement, it is time to set SMART goals. SMART stands for Specific, Measurable, Achievable, Relevant, and Time-bound. Setting SMART goals ensures that your objectives are clear, realistic, and actionable.

For example, if you want to improve your public speaking skills, a SMART goal could be: "I will enroll in a public speaking course and deliver a presentation at work within the next three months." This goal is specific (improving public speaking skills), measurable (delivering a presentation), achievable (enrolling in a course), relevant (for career growth), and time-bound (within three months).

Break down your goals into smaller, manageable steps to

make them more attainable. Celebrate your progress along the way, and don't be afraid to adjust your goals as needed.

7.3.4 Seeking Opportunities for Growth

To develop and grow as an introvert, it is important to seek out opportunities that align with your goals. This may involve stepping out of your comfort zone and challenging yourself in new ways. Look for workshops, seminars, or networking events that can help you develop the skills you want to improve.

Additionally, consider finding a mentor or joining a support group of like-minded individuals. Surrounding yourself with people who understand and appreciate introversion can provide valuable insights, encouragement, and support on your personal growth journey.

7.3.5 Practicing Self-Care and Recharging

While personal growth is important, it is equally crucial to prioritize self-care and recharge as an introvert. Recognize your need for solitude and downtime to recharge your energy. Incorporate activities that bring you joy and relaxation into your personal growth plan.

Whether it's reading a book, going for a walk in nature, practicing mindfulness, or engaging in a creative hobby, make sure to allocate time for activities that nourish your mind, body, and soul. Taking care of yourself will enhance your overall well-being and enable you to show up as your best self in all areas of your life.

7.3.6 Reviewing and Adjusting Your Plan

As you progress on your personal growth journey, regularly review and adjust your plan. Life is dynamic, and your goals and priorities may change over time. Take the time to reflect on your progress, reassess your values and goals, and make any necessary adjustments to your plan.

Remember, personal growth is a lifelong process. Embrace the journey, celebrate your achievements, and be kind to yourself along the way. By developing a personal growth plan as an introvert, you are taking proactive steps to thrive in an extroverted world while staying true to your unique self.

7.4 Celebrating Introversion

Introversion is often misunderstood and undervalued in our society. Many people mistakenly believe that being introverted means there is something wrong with you or that you are somehow less capable than extroverts. However, this couldn't be further from the truth. In fact, introversion is a unique and valuable trait that should be celebrated.

7.4.1 Embracing Individuality

One of the most important aspects of celebrating introversion is embracing individuality. Introverts have their own unique strengths, perspectives, and ways of navigating the world. It is crucial to recognize and appreciate these differences rather than trying to fit into society's extroverted expectations.

7.4.2 The Power of Reflection and Introspection

Introverts have a natural inclination towards reflection and introspection. They often spend time alone, deep in thought, and this allows them to gain a deeper understanding of themselves and the world around them. This ability to reflect and introspect is a powerful tool for personal growth and self-discovery.

7.4.3 Creativity and Imagination

Introverts are known for their creativity and imagination. Their rich inner world allows them to come up with unique ideas and solutions to problems. By celebrating introversion, we can encourage and nurture this creativity, allowing introverts to make valuable contributions to various fields such as art, literature, and science.

7.4.4 Deep Connections and Meaningful Relationships

Introverts may prefer deep and meaningful connections over superficial interactions. They value quality over quantity when it comes to relationships. By celebrating introversion, we can create spaces that allow introverts to form deep connections and foster meaningful relationships with others who appreciate and understand their need for solitude and reflection.

7.4.5 Appreciating the Power of Listening

Introverts are often excellent listeners. They have a natural ability to empathize and understand others. By celebrating introversion, we can encourage and promote the importance of active listening, which is crucial for effective communication and building strong relationships.

7.4.6 Valuing Thoughtful Decision-Making

Introverts tend to think deeply before making decisions. They carefully consider all aspects and weigh the pros and cons. This thoughtful decision-making process often leads to well-informed choices. By celebrating introversion, we can encourage a more thoughtful and deliberate approach to decision-making in our society.

7.4.7 Creating Introvert-Friendly Environments

Celebrating introversion also involves creating introvert-friendly environments. This means providing spaces where introverts can recharge and have moments of solitude without feeling pressured to constantly engage in social interactions. By recognizing and accommodating the needs of introverts, we can create a more inclusive and balanced society.

7.4.8 Challenging Stereotypes and Misconceptions

Another important aspect of celebrating introversion is challenging stereotypes and misconceptions. Introverts are often portrayed as shy, socially awkward, or lacking in social skills. However, introversion is not synonymous with these traits. By educating others and dispelling these misconceptions, we can create a more accurate and positive understanding of introversion.

7.4.9 Promoting Self-Acceptance and Self-Care

Celebrating introversion also involves promoting self-acceptance and self-care among introverts. It is important for introverts to recognize and embrace their unique qualities and needs. By practicing self-care and setting boundaries, introverts can ensure they have the energy and space they need to thrive in an extroverted world.

7.4.10 Fostering a Supportive Community

Lastly, celebrating introversion involves fostering a supportive community for introverts. This can be done through support groups, online communities, or even through organizing events and activities that cater to introverts' preferences. By creating a sense of belonging and understanding, introverts can feel empowered and supported in their journey.

In conclusion, introversion is a valuable and unique trait that should be celebrated. By embracing individuality, appreciating the power of reflection and introspection, nurturing creativity and imagination, valuing deep connections, promoting active listening, and challenging stereotypes, we can create a society that celebrates and supports introverts. By doing so, we can unlock the full potential of introverts and create a more inclusive and balanced world.

8

Chapter 8

The Future for Introversion

8.1 Introverts in a Changing World

Introverts have long been misunderstood and often labeled as "different" or "not like other people." This misconception stems from a lack of understanding about introversion and the unique qualities that introverts possess. However, as the world continues to change and evolve, there is a growing recognition and appreciation for introverts and their valuable contributions.

8.1.1 The Power of Introversion

In a society that often values extroverted traits such as assertiveness and sociability, introverts have faced challenges in being understood and accepted. However, the tide is turning, and the power of introversion is being recognized. Introverts bring a unique set of strengths to the table, including deep thinking, creativity, empathy, and the ability to listen and observe keenly.

8.1.2 The Rise of Introvert Empowerment

With the rise of social media and online platforms, introverts have found new ways to express themselves and connect with others. These platforms provide a space for introverts to share their thoughts, ideas, and experiences without the pressure of face-to-face interactions. As a result, introverts are finding empowerment and a sense of belonging in online communities that understand and appreciate their introverted nature.

8.1.3 Introverts as Leaders and Innovators

Contrary to popular belief, introverts can be highly effective leaders and innovators. Their ability to think deeply and reflect allows them to make thoughtful and well-informed decisions. Introverted leaders often excel in creating inclusive and collaborative work environments, where everyone's ideas are valued and respected. Their quiet confidence and ability to listen attentively make them effective communicators and mentors.

In the rapidly changing world, where adaptability and innovation are crucial, introverts bring a unique perspective. They are often skilled at identifying patterns, analyzing complex problems, and coming up with creative solutions. Their ability to focus deeply on a task allows them to delve into details and uncover insights that others may overlook. As a result, introverts are increasingly being recognized for their contributions to fields such as technology, research, and the arts.

8.1.4 The Importance of Introvert Advocacy

As introverts continue to navigate a world that is predominantly extroverted, it is essential to advocate for their needs and rights. Introvert advocacy involves raising awareness about introversion, challenging stereotypes, and promoting inclusivity. By educating others about introversion and its strengths, we can create a more understanding and accepting society.

Furthermore, organizations and institutions can play a crucial role in supporting introverts by creating environments that cater to their needs. This includes providing quiet spaces for reflection and concentration, offering flexible work arrangements, and valuing diverse communication styles. By embracing introversion and recognizing its value, we can foster a more inclusive and productive society.

8.1.5 Embracing the Changing World

As the world continues to evolve, it is crucial for introverts to embrace the changing landscape and find ways to thrive. This may involve stepping out of their comfort zones and engaging in social interactions that align with their values and interests. It is important for introverts to remember that their unique qualities are assets and that they have much to contribute to the world.

Finding a balance between solitude and social engagement is key for introverts to navigate the changing world successfully. By prioritizing self-care, setting boundaries, and finding meaningful connections, introverts can create a fulfilling and authentic life.

In conclusion, the changing world is gradually recognizing

and appreciating the strengths and contributions of introverts. As introverts continue to advocate for themselves and educate others about introversion, they are paving the way for a more inclusive and understanding society. By embracing their unique qualities and finding their place in the world, introverts can thrive and make a significant impact in their personal and professional lives.

8.2 The Rise of Introvert Empowerment

Introverts have long been misunderstood and often labeled as shy, antisocial, or even aloof. Society has traditionally favored extroverted qualities, valuing outgoing and assertive individuals. However, in recent years, there has been a significant shift in the perception of introversion. The rise of introvert empowerment has brought about a greater understanding and appreciation for the unique strengths and qualities that introverts possess.

8.2.1 Challenging Stereotypes

One of the key aspects of introvert empowerment is challenging the stereotypes and misconceptions that have surrounded introversion for so long. Introverts are often seen as lacking social skills or being unable to thrive in social situations. However, this is far from the truth. Introverts simply have a different way of interacting with the world around them.

Introvert empowerment encourages individuals to embrace their introversion and recognize the inherent strengths that come with it. Rather than trying to conform to extroverted norms, introverts are encouraged to celebrate their unique qualities and find ways to thrive in their own way.

8.2.2 Embracing Authenticity

Introvert empowerment emphasizes the importance of embracing authenticity. In a world that often values surface-level connections and constant social engagement, introverts are encouraged to prioritize deep and meaningful connections. This means being true to oneself and not feeling the need to conform to societal expectations.

By embracing authenticity, introverts can create more fulfilling relationships and experiences. They can focus on building connections that align with their values and interests, rather than trying to fit into social molds that don't resonate with them. This shift towards authenticity is a powerful aspect of introvert empowerment.

8.2.3 Recognizing Strengths

Introvert empowerment also involves recognizing and harnessing the unique strengths that introverts possess. While extroverts may excel in certain areas, introverts have their own set of skills that are equally valuable. Introverts tend to be excellent listeners, deep thinkers, and highly observant individuals.

By recognizing these strengths, introverts can leverage them to their advantage. They can excel in careers that require analytical thinking, creativity, and attention to detail. Introvert empowerment encourages individuals to embrace their strengths and find ways to utilize them in various aspects of their lives.

8.2.4 Creating Introvert-Friendly Spaces

As introvert empowerment continues to gain momentum, there is a growing recognition of the need for introvert-friendly spaces. These are environments that cater to the needs and preferences of introverts, allowing them to recharge and thrive.

Introvert-friendly spaces may include quiet areas for reflection and solitude, flexible work arrangements that allow for focused work, and opportunities for meaningful one-on-one interactions. By creating these spaces, organizations and communities can foster an inclusive environment that values and supports introverts.

8.2.5 Amplifying Introvert Voices

Another important aspect of introvert empowerment is the amplification of introvert voices. Historically, extroverted voices have dominated public discourse and leadership positions. However, introverts have unique perspectives and insights that deserve to be heard.

Introvert empowerment encourages introverts to step into leadership roles and share their ideas and experiences. By doing so, introverts can contribute to a more balanced and diverse society. It is through the amplification of introvert voices that a more inclusive and understanding world can be created.

8.2.6 Fostering Collaboration

Introvert empowerment also emphasizes the importance of collaboration. While introverts may thrive in solitude, they also have the ability to work effectively in teams. By recognizing and valuing the contributions of introverts, organizations can create a collaborative environment that brings together the strengths of both introverts and extroverts.

By fostering collaboration, introvert empowerment encourages the exchange of ideas and the creation of innovative solutions. It recognizes that introverts have unique perspectives and approaches that can greatly contribute to the success of a team or organization.

8.2.7 The Power of Introvert Advocacy

Introvert empowerment goes beyond individual growth and extends to advocacy for introverts as a whole. It involves raising awareness about introversion, challenging stereotypes, and promoting inclusivity. Introvert advocacy aims to create a society that values and respects introverts, providing equal opportunities for success and personal fulfillment.

Through advocacy, introverts can come together to support and uplift each other. They can share their experiences, offer guidance, and create a sense of community. Introvert empowerment and advocacy work hand in hand to create a world where introverts can thrive and be celebrated for who they are.

In conclusion, the rise of introvert empowerment signifies a shift in societal attitudes towards introversion. It challenges stereotypes, embraces authenticity, recognizes strengths, creates introvert-friendly spaces, amplifies introvert voices, fosters collaboration, and advocates for introverts. By empowering introverts, we can create a more inclusive and understanding world that values the unique qualities and contributions of introverted individuals.

8.3 Introverts as Leaders and Innovators

Introverts have long been misunderstood and overlooked in the realm of leadership and innovation. The extroverted ideal has dominated our society's perception of what a leader should be - someone outgoing, charismatic, and assertive. However, as we delve deeper into the intricacies of introversion, we begin to realize that introverts possess unique qualities that make them exceptional leaders and innovators.

8.3.1 The Strengths of Introverted Leaders

Introverted leaders bring a different set of strengths to the table that can greatly benefit organizations and teams. One of the key strengths of introverted leaders is their ability to listen attentively. They have a natural inclination to listen and observe, allowing them to gather valuable insights and perspectives from their team members. This empathetic listening creates an environment where individuals feel heard and valued, fostering trust and collaboration.

Another strength of introverted leaders is their thoughtful and strategic approach to decision-making. They tend to carefully analyze information, weigh different options, and consider the long-term implications of their choices. This deliberate decision-making process often leads to well-thought-out and effective strategies.

Introverted leaders also excel in creating a calm and focused work environment. Their preference for solitude and reflection allows them to create spaces where individuals can concentrate and work independently. This quiet and introspective atmosphere can enhance productivity and creativity, enabling team members to generate innovative ideas and solutions.

8.3.2 The Power of Introverted Innovators

Innovation requires a deep understanding of complex problems and the ability to think critically. Introverts possess these qualities in abundance. Their introspective nature allows them to delve into the depths of a problem, analyzing it from various angles and considering all possible solutions. This analytical mindset often leads to breakthrough innovations that address the root causes of problems.

Introverted innovators also excel in their ability to focus deeply on a task or project. They have a natural inclination to immerse themselves in their work, shutting out distractions and honing their attention to detail. This intense focus allows them to uncover hidden patterns, identify opportunities, and develop innovative solutions.

Furthermore, introverted innovators thrive in environments that provide them with the necessary solitude and autonomy to explore their ideas. They often prefer working independently or in small, focused teams where they can fully immerse themselves in their work. This freedom to explore and experiment without constant external stimulation can lead to groundbreaking discoveries and inventions.

8.3.3 Overcoming Misconceptions and Embracing Introverted Leadership

Despite the strengths and abilities of introverted leaders and innovators, they often face misconceptions and biases in the workplace. The extroverted ideal still prevails, leading to the undervaluing of introverted qualities and the overlooking of introverted individuals for leadership positions.

To overcome these misconceptions, organizations need to recognize and appreciate the unique strengths that introverted leaders bring to the table. They should create inclusive environments that value diverse perspectives and provide opportunities for introverts to thrive. This can be achieved by implementing flexible work arrangements, promoting a culture of deep listening and collaboration, and providing spaces for quiet reflection and focused work.

Additionally, introverted individuals themselves can take steps to embrace their leadership potential. They can develop their communication and networking skills, leveraging their natural ability to listen and observe to build meaningful connections. They can also seek out mentors and role models who exemplify successful introverted leadership, learning from their experiences and strategies.

8.3.4 The Future of Introverted Leadership and Innovation

As our society continues to evolve, there is a growing recognition of the value that introverted leaders and innovators bring to the table. Organizations are beginning to understand that diverse leadership styles, including introverted ones, can lead to more balanced and effective decision-making.

The future holds great potential for introverted leaders and innovators to thrive. With the rise of remote work and virtual collaboration, introverts can leverage their strengths in deep thinking, focused work, and empathetic listening to excel in these new environments. The digital age also provides platforms for introverted individuals to share their ideas and innovations with a wider audience, amplifying their impact.

Furthermore, as introverted individuals continue to advocate for their strengths and challenge societal misconceptions, we can expect to see a shift in the perception of introversion. Introverted leaders and innovators will be celebrated for their unique contributions, and organizations will actively seek out their expertise and insights.

In conclusion, introverted individuals possess a wealth of strengths and qualities that make them exceptional leaders and innovators. Their ability to listen attentively, think critically, and create focused work environments sets them apart. By embracing and valuing introverted leadership, we can create a more inclusive and innovative future.

8.4 The Importance of Introvert Advocacy

Introversion is often misunderstood and overlooked in a society that values extroverted traits and behaviors. Many introverts have experienced the frustration of being labeled as shy, anti-social, or even aloof simply because they prefer solitude and introspection over constant social interaction. This lack of understanding can lead to feelings of isolation and a sense of not belonging.

Advocacy for introverts is crucial in order to challenge these misconceptions and promote a more inclusive and accepting society. By advocating for introverts, we can raise awareness about the unique strengths and needs of introverted individuals, and create a world that values and respects introversion as an equally valid personality trait.

8.4.1 Challenging Stereotypes and Misconceptions

One of the key aspects of introvert advocacy is challenging the stereotypes and misconceptions that surround introversion. Many people mistakenly believe that introverts are shy, socially awkward, or lacking in social skills. However, introversion is not synonymous with these traits. Introverts simply gain energy from solitude and introspection, and may prefer deeper, more meaningful connections over superficial small talk.

Advocacy efforts can involve educating others about the true nature of introversion and dispelling these stereotypes. By sharing personal stories and experiences, introverts can help others understand that introversion is not a flaw or a weakness, but rather a unique way of processing the world.

8.4.2 Promoting Inclusivity and Understanding

Introvert advocacy also aims to promote inclusivity and understanding in various social settings. This includes workplaces, schools, and social events where introverts may feel pressured to conform to extroverted norms. By advocating for the needs of introverts, we can encourage the creation of environments that cater to different personality types and allow introverts to thrive.

In workplaces, for example, introvert advocacy can involve advocating for flexible work arrangements that allow for periods of solitude and uninterrupted focus. It can also involve promoting the value of introverted traits such as deep thinking, careful analysis, and creativity, which are often overlooked in favor of more extroverted qualities.

8.4.3 Fostering Self-Acceptance and Empowerment

Advocacy for introverts also plays a crucial role in fostering self-acceptance and empowerment among introverted individuals. Many introverts have internalized societal messages that suggest they need to change or "fix" themselves in order to fit in. This can lead to feelings of inadequacy and a constant struggle to conform to extroverted expectations.

By advocating for introverts, we can help introverted individuals embrace their true selves and recognize the unique strengths they bring to the table. This can involve providing resources, support, and guidance to help introverts navigate social situations, build confidence, and develop strategies for self-care.

8.4.4 Creating a More Balanced Society

Advocacy for introverts is not about diminishing the value of extroversion, but rather about creating a more balanced and inclusive society that values and respects both introverted and extroverted individuals. By advocating for introverts, we can challenge the notion that extroversion is the ideal or superior personality type, and instead promote the understanding that both introversion and extroversion have their own strengths and contributions to offer.

A more balanced society recognizes that introverts have

unique perspectives, insights, and talents that can enrich various aspects of life, including creativity, innovation, problem-solving, and leadership. By advocating for introverts, we can create spaces where introverted individuals feel valued, understood, and empowered to contribute their unique gifts to the world.

8.4.5 The Power of Introvert Advocacy

Introvert advocacy has the power to create a more inclusive and understanding society, where introverts are celebrated for their unique qualities and contributions. By challenging stereotypes, promoting inclusivity, fostering self-acceptance, and creating a more balanced society, introvert advocacy can help introverted individuals thrive and reach their full potential.

It is important for introverts to find their voice and actively participate in advocacy efforts. By sharing their stories, experiences, and insights, introverts can help educate others and create a more empathetic and accepting world. Together, introverts and extroverts can work towards building a society that values and celebrates the diversity of personality types, ultimately leading to a more harmonious and fulfilling existence for all.

About the Author

Sara grew up in a small coastal town in the Hunter Valley region in N.S.W, Australia. She experienced sexism, homophobia, and the pressure to conform to hetero-normative standards of the time; at home, at school and by the parochial attitudes of the local coastal community. She moved to the big city to find freedom, develop her long held passions, create change and develop her authentic self. She has studied clinical and forensic psychology, taught at university and worked in community corrections.

www.ingramcontent.com/pod-product-compliance
Lightning Source LLC
Chambersburg PA
CBHW070531160726
48003CB00004B/1756